We
Are
Our
Past

A link with Ireland's Past

Doreen McBride

ADARE PRESS
White Gables
Ballymoney Hill
Banbridge
Telephone: Banbridge 23782

© 1990 Doreen McBride
Published by Adare Press
Typeset by Hallographics, Belfast
Printed by Romac Ltd., Belfast

ISBN 0 9516686 0 9

CONTENTS

"You may not realise it, but the blood of saints and scholars runs in my veins."

Chapter 1

WE ARE OUR PAST

This book is an exploration of my past, aspects of which are shared by everyone of Irish descent. It includes things I have seen and heard, the memories of people I know, people from every walk of life and all sides of the community and the places involved.

There have been more changes in the past hundred years than there have been in the previous thousand. If Rip Van Winkle had gone to sleep in 1890 and wakened up in 1990 think of his surprise and perhaps his horror! Aeroplanes, motor cars, electric light, fires and stoves, washing machines, tumbler dryers, radio and television. Think of the way the landscape has changed, the change in house types, to say nothing of central heating, modern plumbing, modern sewage works, hospitals, modern medicine and good water supplies piped into buildings.

I remember my grandmother sitting by the fire talking to my mother. 'It is a poor summer,' she said, 'hunger will stalk the land.' At the time I thought that was just granny's old fashioned talk and dismissed it. Now I am not so sure. I feel we have a lot to be thankful for. Thanks to state benefits today nobody faces the prospect of starving to death. It is a sobering thought that in Belfast in the 1850s the average expectancy of life was 29 years. Life expectancy throughout Europe was low, until people were provided with safe water supplies, and efficient means of sewage disposal.

Estyn Evans suggested that each person has folk memories, unconscious feelings that have been passed down from generation to generation. It may be fanciful, but I believe it to be true. I feel extra satisfaction as I tend my fire, that old fashioned source of heat and comfort much loved by Irish people, realising that I am responding to a distant folk memory of days and nights spent around the fire enjoying 'good crack'*

* 'crack' means conversation in Ireland.

I was intrigued by the reactions of some Americans of Irish descent to my fire. They loved it! The sat up close saying they could imagine their ancestors sitting around a fire such as that in the past. Perhaps Irish folk memories are present in all the corners of the world containing Irish emigrants? At any rate, it is true to say that each individual is under the influence of his, or her, past. The past includes half forgotten memories of childhood and the family's oral history, which shapes attitudes, even if the reason for those attitudes is subconscious. To a large extent we are our past.

Old fireplace adapted for use today. Laurelvale, Moy, County Tyrone.

Chapter 2

HOME IS WHERE
THE HEARTH IS

Like the majority of people, my attitudes were formed at home. Evenings sitting around the ever-important fire left a lasting impression. The atmosphere created by the flickering flames is entirely absent from our, admittedly more comfortable, centrally heated homes. The Irish are a nation of home lovers and it is interesting to see how these homes have changed over the centuries

In Ireland the earliest homes were round, or rectangular structures. Many homes were built on crannogs. A crannog was an artificial island built in a lake. Many crannogs had underwater 'causeways' made from woven reeds. These causeways were held in position by wooden structures which looked like modern tent pegs. People living on the crannog knew where the causeway was situated. They escaped from enemies by running across the causeway, then pulling it behind them. Crannogs were used from about 1200 B.C. — 1700 A.D.

Early homes were made from wood on a wooden frame with a closely woven wickerwork of hazel or birch. Two walls were built

Crannog, Loughbrickland, 1989.

Reconstruction of a Crannog, History Park, Gortin, County Tyrone, 1990.

in close proximity, the space between the walls was filled with heather as insulation, the spaces in the wickerwork were filled by mud and daub.

The fireplace was important in the earliest homes. If the mud fell off the walls the wooden frame was uncovered and could catch fire, so the fireplace was set in the middle of the building, with a hole in the roof above it to let the smoke out. Round houses had the highest point of the roof in the centre of the building. Rectangular houses had a central ridgepole running along the length of the house so that the highest point of the roof was also in the centre. A central fire, with the highest point of the roof above it, was less likely to burn the house down than one set against a wall.

A central hearth had other advantages. It warmed the whole house, not just one corner. People could sit in a circle around it and each person had a fair share of the heat. During dark winter evenings people could sit around and indulge in 'crack', that is, conversation, something which Irish people love. If the conversation was particularly good it was referred to as 'quare crack'. People also told stories around the fire and this led to Ireland's rich tradition of story telling. At the end of an evening's 'crack' people slept in a circle on the bare floor around the fire with their feet pointing towards it.

There used to be a railway station at Ashleigh, near Dromore in County Down. It had a fire in the centre of its waiting room. Old age pensioners around the district recall the 'crack' around that particular fire. During the winter time people used to come from miles around to sit around the fire and chat. Apparently most of them had no intention of going anywhere. They just enjoyed the company in the railway station with its undertones of folk memory.

Chimneyless houses must have been full of smoke. Look at Moffat's description of the house that belonged to the Irish hero called Gillo.

> 'And when the occasion did require
> In midst of house a mighty fire
> Of black dry'd earth and swinging blocks,
> Was made enough to roast an ox,
> From which arose such clouds of smoak,
> As either you or me would choak,
> But Gillo and his train inur'd

To smoak, the same with ease endur'd,
By sitting low on rushes spread,
The smoak still hovere'd overhead,
And did more good than real harm,
Because it kept the long house warme
And never made their heads to ake,
Therefore no chimney he would make
And thus for smoak altho' twas dear,
He paid four shillings every year.'

Gillo paid four shillings every year for his smoke because in 1662 the Hearth Money Act was passed. He must have had two chimneys because the Hearth Money Act was a house tax rather than a poll tax. It placed a tax of two shillings on every hearth, fireplace or stove in all houses which had an annual valuation of more than eight shillings. It was said that the Irish were willing to pay extra for smoke because they thought 'it nourisheth and keepeth warme their children.' Chimney smoke was believed to have a good effect until well into the twentieth century.

Sitting on a creepy or stool.

Traditionally on Saturday night the family pulled a zinc bath in front of the fire, filled it with water and had a bath.

I remember in July 1963 I visited Grace Kerr, an old lady who lived in Ahoghill, County Antrim. She was a great old lady, well into her eighties, who lived in a tiny, traditional house untouched by any attempt at modernisation. She bade us very welcome and drew 'creepie' stools up to the fire to make us comfortable. The fireplace was set in the wall furthest from the door and at right-angles to it. It had an open hearth and a crook on which pots and kettles were hung. Grace arranged the kettle on the crook and swung it over the fire asking us if we would like a cup of tea. As I drank my tea, I gazed up the chimney at the sky and began to cough and splutter because of the dense smoke inside the house. Grace, and other locals who had come in for a chat, laughed at my discomfort saying that 'townies are all the same. They can't stand a drop of smoke' and 'Smoke is good for you. Do you not know it is very nourishing?' Later I was mortified to overhear two elderly gentlemen discussing me. 'That wee girl,' they said, 'will not make much of a wife. She's too small and not broad enough to be able to pull a plough. And did you hear her cough? She'll catch T.B. and die young, I'm telling you. She's useless!'

Although she was old, Grace's house was tidy and well ordered. She had the traditional buckets of water standing inside the door. She explained that it was unlucky to go to bed at night without making sure that there was plenty of water stored for the next day. Grace told me she washed her feet very carefully before going to bed at night. She said it was unlucky not to throw out water in which feet had been washed. It was possible to share foot water provided that after each person had finished using the water in turn, a piece of hot coal from the fire was picked up with the fire tongs and dropped in the water. Grace told me she was always careful to empty it into the drain outside. She never simply threw it outside the door because that could annoy the fairies and bring bad luck.

Keeping clean was a real problem without a supply of running water. Water had to be carried from the well in buckets, which were usually left standing inside the door of the house, beside the wall. This water was carefully hoarded and used several times. Water, in which potatoes had been boiled, was saved and used to wash dishes, hands or clothes before being thrown out.

Saturday night was traditionally 'bath night'. A zinc bath, or a waterproof wooden tub, was pulled out in front of the fire, filled with water heated in kettles over the fire, and used by each member of the family. Grace said her family started with the youngest child and ended with the eldest, washing each one in turn and putting it to bed 'out of the road. 'Once the children were finished her mother had her bath followed by her father. The bath water was saved to wash clothes if it looked at all clean. Grace said, rather sadly, once the water had been used to wash the whole family it was usually very dirty and had to be thrown out.

Carrying water was a back breaking job. There is an old saying in County Tyrone — 'She is a great girl. Her back is broad enough to carry two buckets!'

Grace lifted an old framed photograph off the wall to show me. We carried it over to the door to look at it more closely in a good light. It was covered by a thin layer of soot. Grace began to rub the glass with a duster. 'It's terrible hard to keep the stour down.' she said. I shudder to think what life must have been like inside a house which did not have a chimney.

It is thought that the first chimneys in Ireland were built by monks in the monasteries and by the Anglo Normans, in their castles such as that at Carrickfergus. It is believed that these early chimneys did not have much impact on the local population because very few people were allowed to visit either a monastery or a castle. Also, it would have been difficult to adapt the idea of a stone chimney built into the wall of a stone house into a structure that was suitable for use in a house with flammable wattle walls and a central hearth.

'Forest chimneys' are believed to be the first chimneys to be built into ordinary local homes. They were made in the form of a four-sided funnel, held up by two parallel cross beams, built over the central hearth. They were made of lath, or wattle work, coated with daub. If the daub fell off the inner surface of the chimney the wooden framework was exposed and it could catch fire. Forest chimneys were very dangerous and had a tendency to burn the house down. It is thought that over the course of time they were replaced by those made of brick or stone. This led to the development of the traditional house type with the fireplace built against an inner wall.

Some new houses were built without chimneys up until the end of the nineteenth century.

Sometimes improving landlords caused bad feeling by building chimneys inside tenants' houses. In 1868 Lord Lorton, who had an estate at Rockingham, County Roscommon, decided to improve the houses on his property. He built chimneys. His tenants were furious. They sent a deputation to his lordship asking that the chimneys be destroyed because they made the houses cold. The heat of the fire escaped through the chimney along with the smoke. Chimneys throughout Ireland were blocked up by tenants because they believed the smoke warmed them although it hurt the womens' eyes as they cooked over the fire and it made their skin resemble smoked ham.

Would your Lordship please remove those newfangled chimneys and give us back our smoke?

In Ireland the simplest form of house had one room. The door was placed in the same wall as the window. The chimney and hearth could be found in one of two places, either on the wall adjacent to the door, or on the opposite wall, that is, on the wall adjacent to the window away from the door. Most houses had only one door.

Houses were built from local materials. They were made from mud sods, or turf, or stone, or clay. The poorest houses were made from sods of mud or sods of turf. They were quick and easy to build. They housed most of the population during the early part of the nineteenth century. At that time the population was still growing rapidly. Small holdings were divided and sub-divided with smaller and smaller fields. Houses had to be built quickly and cheaply. Sods were cut out of the earth, or from the bogs in the shape of bricks. The sods were used to build walls and the roof was thatched with materials common locally such as straw or marram grass. Unfortunately sod houses did not have a very long life. Within ten years the walls began to bulge and threatened to fall down, as a result of rain and damp, so the occupants propped them up with

13

Before the Great Famine most of the population of Ireland lived in houses built from sods.

branches of trees, or anything else that happened to be handy. This type of house practically disappeared when the Great Famine decimated the population.

Byre houses have also disappeared in Ireland. They used to be common along the Alantic coast of Europe, including Ireland. In a byre dwelling the people lived at one end of the house, the cows at the other. The cows were not separated from the people by a wall.

Cows were tied to posts at one end of the room during the winter time. A trench cut into the floor caught their droppings. A hole in the wall of the house at the bottom of the trench let liquid flow out of the house. This kept the trench from overflowing. People living inside byre houses cleaned them out once a year removing between ten and twelve tons of manure. This manure was very, very precious because it increased crop yield. A farmer with three acres of land and a cow could feed six people. He would have divided his land into three parts. One part would have been used to grow oats, the second grass and the third potatoes. Crops were rotated each year.

The farmer and his family ate potatoes and oats. They drank the cow's milk. The cow ate grass during the summer and oats during the winter. It produced manure to fertilise the ground. On Festive occasions the farmer cut one of the cow's veins and collected blood

End of byre house, Ulster Folk and Transport Museum where cows were housed.

Cow, near Leitrim in the Mourne Country, grazing by roadside. April 1990.

from it in a bucket. The blood was mixed with oatmeal and used to make black sausages or to give a meaty flavour to Irish Stew to provide a delicacy for the festive occasion.

There is a very interesting tape in the archives of the Ulster Folk and Transport Museum. It was made by an old man who had farmed in County Donegal. He explained on the tape the terrible effect the death of his cow had had on his family. When the cow died it obviously could not produce manure! The family went ahead and planted potatoes at the usual time without fertilising the soil with manure. At harvest time they 'dug all day' but did not have sufficient potatoes to carry home on their backs. Faced with starvation the farmer left his family and travelled to Scotland. He found work and was able to send money home to keep his family from starving and to save up and buy a new cow.

The milk cow was very precious and was treated as one of the family. The fire was believed to give protection from evil spirits so, in a byre house, it was only proper that the cow should have a glimpse of it. Churning was done in front of the fire and the grain was stored inside the house. The single room inside the byre house acted as a byre, a living room and a granary.

Byre houses were unusual compared to other traditional house types in Ireland. They had two doors, one at the front of the house and the other opposite it at the back. These opposite doors formed a passageway through the house. Cows were usually milked inside the house and the two doors allowed them to be driven straight through.

Grain was threshed inside the house, just inside the door. This gave rise to the word 'threshold'. The other door was left open to allow a draft of air which blew the light outer covering, or chaff, of the seeds away.

Byre houses were very unhealthy places in which to live. The occupants caught fleas, lice, ticks and other parasites from cows, as well as more serious diseases such as tuberculosis and brucellosis. Needless to say cows also caught these diseases from humans.

Poor people did not have beds. They slept on the bare floor, or on a straw-filled bag called a 'shake down', or on straw. Colm Barton remembers a boy who went to the school he attended as a child. The boy was blind in one eye. His pupil was completely white because he came from a poor family and slept on straw. A piece of straw stuck into his eye and blinded him.

Some houses had a half loft, that is a floor built on top of the walls under the roof space. The half loft covered about half of the roof space. It was used as a store and the children were lifted up into it to sleep at night.

An outshoot was frequently built into the wall near the fire, forming a place to sleep. Traditionally old people, or any member of the family who was ill, slept in the bed outshoot because it was warm and snug.

Larger houses had bedrooms. The basic house type was extended in a straight line with the bedroom opening off the main living room. In some parts of the country it was believed to be unlucky to extend the house on its west side because fairies made paths to the west of human dwellings. Woe betide the inhabitants if they interfered with a fairy path!

Another means of extending a traditional house was to build a second storey on top of the ground floor. This was called 'raising the house'. If the house was 'raised' the bedrooms were moved

Laurelvale, Moy, County Tyrone. The heart of this house is a single roomed dwelling with mud walls. It has been extended and 'raised'.

Jam wall inside door.

Half door.

upstairs. Corridors did not exist. Rooms simply opened off each other.

There was a tax on glass so windows in traditional houses were few and small. This led to the habit of leaving the door open to let light in and to provide ventilation. Traditionally Irish people are very helpful and friendly. An open door was regarded as a sign of welcome although it must have been cold in the winter time. This tradition persists in rural areas today. The door may be shut in deference to modern ideas on central heating, but unlocked. Visitors are encouraged to open it and walk in to the house. In country towns, in spite of advice about the advisability of keeping burglars out, people often leave the key in the lock of the front door so that friends and relations may walk in.

A wide open door caused draughts, particularly if the fire was adjacent to it. This led to the construction of jam walls. A jam wall was a short wall inside the door. It protected the fire from the draught caused by the open door. Jam walls often had a small window so that the farmer's wife could peep out as she worked at the fire to see who was at the door.

At times an open door was a bit of an nuisance as farm animals and young children could walk in and out at will. This inconvenience led to the invention of the 'half door'. The 'half door' was a door which was cut into two so that the bottom portion could remain shut while the top was opened to give light and ventilation.

According to Irish folk lore it is extremely unlucky to destroy an old house because the spirits of the people who lived there in the past become lost and feel unhappy. Old houses were allowed to decay slowly and only after they were derelict were stones from them used to mend dry stone walls or for other purposes. Even today Ireland is littered with old houses that are slowly crumbling.

Irish folk lore also suggests that at night, when the people in the house are asleep, the souls of the old people, that is, the people who lived there in the past, come back. They sit around the fire and contentedly indulge in a bit of crack.

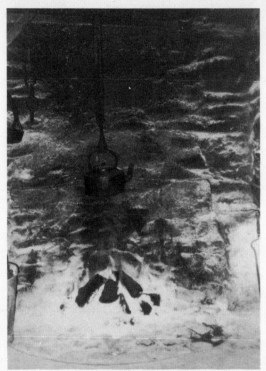

Kettle suspended over fire.

Cooking utensils used in the past. Ulster Folk and Transport Museum.

Chapter 3

THE HOME, THE HEARTH AND ALL

The fire warmed the whole house. It also served as a source of heat for cooking, a place to boil the washing, to dry and air clothes, a light source and a focal point for the family and their visitors.

The fire acted as a sign of family continuity because it was never allowed to go out. The housewife tended it last thing at night, pouring ashes over turf embers so that they smouldered quietly until morning when a few rakings with the poker and the use of bellows brought it to life again. Turf, also called peat, cut from the bogs was the most common fuel. Blocks of wood and coal were used in places where bogs were scarce or supplied poor quality turf. Coal was used in parts of the east and of the north. It was virtually unknown in the west and the south.

Gorse, also called whin or furze, was sometimes used as a fuel. It burned very quickly and provided good heat. A favourite way to clean a chimney was to drop a rope down it then tie a gorse bush to the end of it. The rope was then pulled up and down the chimney knocking the soot off.

Children were expected to collect sticks used to make the fire light up quickly in the morning. Each child was expected to collect a large bundle and leave it in a basket beside the fire for use the following morning.

Most open hearths had cranes, or crooks, which were used for cooking. The crane was set in the recess at the left of the fire. Pots were suspended from it on hooks called pot hangers. The woman of the house was able to swing the crane, with its suspended pots, over the fire using her left hand. Her right hand was free to stir the contents of the pots. Traditionally the woman sat on the left of the fire so that she was convenient to the crane. The man sat on the right.

An old friend, in her ninetieth year, told me that now she loves looking at her hands because they are clean. In the past, when she cooked over an open fire her hands became ingrained with soot and always appeared filthy.

It was possible to say how wealthy a household was by looking at the number of cooking pots they owned. The greater the number of cooking pots the wealthier the household. A poor house would have possessed one pot while a rich house would have possessed a whole array of different sized cooking pots, a kettle and a pot oven. A pot oven was a legless pot with a flat lid. A few embers were poked out of the fire onto one side of the hearth. The pot oven was placed on them and the lid covered with glowing embers. Pot ovens were used to bake bread. Griddle bread was baked on a griddle, that is a flat round iron plate with a handle to suspend it from the crane.

Crickets were encouraged to live around the fireplace. Crickets are insects that look like grasshoppers. A cricket on the hearth was regarded as a sign of good luck. The housewife used a goose wing to spread flour on her griddle before baking potato bread, soda bread, oat cakes and scones. As she spread the flour over the griddle she would flick some on to the hearth to feed the crickets. A good fire, the kettle on the boil and a cricket singing on the hearth represented the soul of comfort and contentment.

Goose wing in jar beside baking bowl.

22

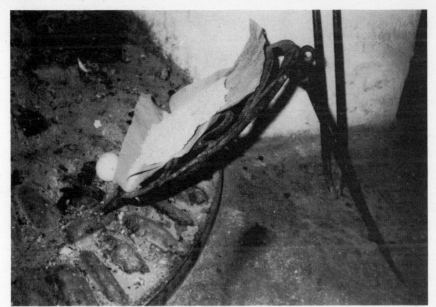

Oat cakes drying on a bread stand (also called a hamen). Sometimes oat cakes were dried resting on paper as shown. Bread stands were also used without paper.

I remember as a very young child being taken to vist my mother's old Aunt Bella who lived near Ballynure. Aunt Bella was thrilled because a cricket came out and sang on the hearth. I, much to everyones great annoyance, burst into tears. I can remember thinking it was a dirty looking thing and being very upset that it was so near the food I was expected to eat. 'Is that cricket not covered in germs?' I sobbed. Aunt Bella laughed and laughed. 'That's not a dirty thing like a clock*', she said. 'It's very lucky to see a cricket and you should be laughing, not crying, so dry your eyes and stop blubbering!'

Once the bread was baked it was popped up on a bread stand near the fire to dry out. Bread stands were also used to make toast.

In the old days the country kitchen was very different from that found in modern homes. Before the invention of electricity light was at a premium so the kitchen table was never placed in the centre of the floor. It was set in front of the window so that the farmer's wife would have the greatest amount of light possible as she worked.

* *A black beetle. Aunt Bella believed that insects, such as houseflies, fleas, cockroaches, etc., which could pass disease to humans were 'dirty'. All other insects were 'clean.'*

"Come on, on in and I'll give you a wee cup of tea in your hand."

Traditional house, Donegal, August 1989.

Families who lived in single roomed houses probably did not have a table. They ate around a large cooking pot. Once the potatoes were cooked they were strained through a large strainer made from wickerware and shaped like a plate with a rim around the edge. The potatoes were placed on the strainer and covered with a clean cloth. The water that was strained off the potatoes was saved and put back in the pot. The steam arising from it kept the potatoes warm. After the meal was finished the water was used to wash the dishes. The family sat around the pot and helped themselves to potatoes. Each member of the family had his, or her, own special place around the cooking pot.

Most families ate out of bowls. The bowls could be filled with soup, or stew, then washed and used for drinking tea.

In Ireland today it is still possible to be invited to 'Come and have a wee cup of tea in your hand.' This means to have a drink of tea while sitting beside the fire without anyone going to the trouble of laying a formal table.

Rich families had separate dining rooms and a wealth of china in contrast to the majority of smallholders who had a single room to serve as a kitchen, a dining room, a bed room and a place in which to wash.

The rooms in homes belonging to smallholders tended to be small so furniture was placed around the walls to avoid cluttering the middle of the floor. Traditionally the dresser was placed against the wall opposite the fire. It was used to display the family's china. Some families had a dresser that held the family china in the top section and hens in the bottom section. A dresser of this type may be seen at Bunratty Folk Park, County Limerick.

The fire was the only source of light for poor families. Candles were expensive items. The simplest type of candle was made by dipping rushes in wax. The rush acted as a wick and the wax prevented it from burning too quickly. Sometimes a family would make a pledge to keep a candle lit in the window during the hours of darkness until one of its absent members returned. This represented a considerable sacrifice because candles were so expensive.

Candles were gradually replaced by oil lamps. Today the majority of houses have electric light. I remember in 1973 a woman in Gilford, County Down, saying that she had recently persuaded her father, to put electricity into their farmhouse. She said that she found life was much easier with electric light. She had not realised how much time she had spent preparing the oil lamps for service.

Traditional farmhouse, near Newcastle, County Down, April 1990.

Chapter 4

THE GREAT HUNGER

The Antrim Coast road stretches from Larne to Cushendall. It is a beautiful yet, like many other places in Ireland, this was the site of appalling tragedy. People starved to death in this beautiful place. There is a memorial carved into the limestone on the landward side of the road, about a quarter of a mile north-west of Garron Point, near Carnlough. It is known as the 'Famine Stone'.

FRANCES ANNE VANE
MARCHIONESS OF LONDONDERRY
BEING CONNECTED WITH THIS PROVINCE
BY THE DOUBLE TIES OF BIRTH AND MARRIAGE
AND BEING DESIROUS TO HAND DOWN TO PROSPERITY
AN IMPERISHABLE MEMORIAL TO IRELAND'S AFFLICTION
AND ENGLAND'S GENEROSITY
IN THE YEAR 1846-47
UNPARALLELED IN THE ANNALS OF HUMAN SUFFERING
HATH ENGRAVED THIS STONE
Fair tablet fashioned by the Almighty's Hand
To guard these confines of the sea and land
No longer shalt thou meet the stranger's sight,
A polished surface of unmeaning white,
But bid him ponder on the days of yore,
When plague and famine stalked along the shore,
And oale Irene veiled her drooping head,
Like Rachel weeping for her children dead,
Tell him to assuage these pangs and fears
Britannia gave her bounty with her tears
And hear this record, though in phrases crude,
Of England's love and Ireland's gratitude.
Inscription on the 'Famine Stone', Antrim Coast Road.

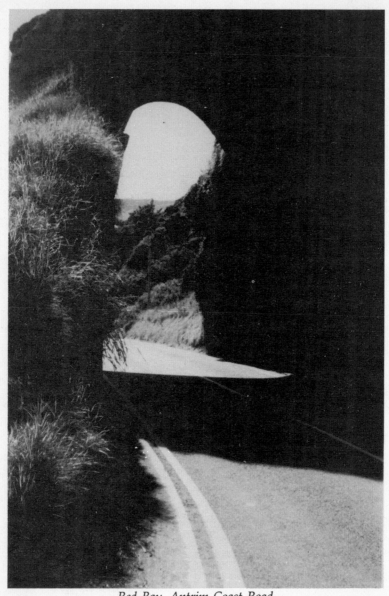

Red Bay, Antrim Coast Road.

People with nationalistic sympathies destroyed part of the text during the 1920s. Some time afterwards a bronze plaque was placed beside the original text. The plaque contains a transcription of the original message.

What happened? Why is there reference to plague and famine?

Local folk lore suggests that the road was built during a terrible famine in 1833. The road was supposed to provide a means for starving people to earn food and that payment for a day's work was a small bowl of rice. It is said that forty people, men, women and children died for each mile of the road constructed.

How did such a tragedy happen? What caused it?

There were many famines in Ireland and a devastating one (1846-47) which became known as the 'great hunger'. The history of the famines is very complicated. All areas were not affected equally.

Famines were caused by failure of potato crops.

Potatoes formed the staple diet of people in poorer areas. Meat was rarely eaten except at Easter or Christmas. Families could not afford to eat meat and even those who reared a pig were forced to sell it to pay the rent.

Potatoes, with the addition of milk or buttermilk, form a scientifically balanced diet. Poor people who did not have enough to eat undercooked their potatoes because hard, undercooked potatoes are more difficult to digest than soft ones. They stay in the stomach for a longer time and cut down the number of hunger pains felt.

The potato crop failed because of potato blight fungus, Phytophthora infestans. Spores of the fungus landed on the potato leaves, grew down through a leaf pore and rapidly killed the plant. If rain washed the fungus off the leaves it entered the ground and attacked potato tubers so that they became rotten.

During the eighteenth and early nineteenth centuries Ireland's population grew rapidly. Most people lived at subsistence level. They found day to day existence difficult and had no resources to help them survive a misfortune.

The 1842 census nearly half of the rural population lived in sod houses. The evicted and those who were unable to get work dug holes in banks, and lived in them; existed in bogholes and put roofs made of branches over ditches.

Cave, Red Bay, Antrim Coast Road. This cave was once occupied.

Many people fell into debt. Middle men who collected debt were called 'gombeen men'. I remember being very naughty as a small child and my grandmother saying to me 'You'd better be a good girl or the gombeen man will get you.' I had no idea what a gombeen man was but the menace reflected in my grandmother's voice sounded terrifying and I behaved. People falling in arrears with their debt were evicted. Eviction removed them from their homes and their livelihood. They were left to starve to death because there was no state benefit. Evicted people had nowhere to go but the workhouse. According to my grandmother, that was a fate worse than death.

The Irish are fond of children. In the days before old age pensions children acted as insurance against destitution in old age. Children

Gate of the now derelict workhouse, Dunfanaghy, Co. Donegal, August 1989.

were expected to look after their parents, to run the farm and do their best to ensure that aged parents did not suffer want. Large families were normal.

The demand for land increased as the population grew. Farms which had been divided by middlemen and landlords were divided again by the people themselves. Parents allowed their children to have a portion of their land because the alternative was to turn them out to starve. These children in their turn allowed their children to use their land. In a comparatively short time many families were settled on land that could only provide food for one family. Competition for land caused the rents to become high.

In the mid-nineteenth century there had been no scientific breeding of potatoes and as a result most potato crops were prone to disease. There had been many crop failures over the years. In 1821 and 1822 the potato crop failed in Munster and Connaught while in 1832, 1833, 1834 and 1836 a large number of districts had poor potato crops because of the diseases known as potato dry rot and potato leafcurl.

In 1845 the potato crop looked as if it was going to be good. On 25th July 1845 'The Times' reported that an early harvest was expected. When the potatoes came to be harvested they appeared good but they turned into a stinking mass within days. This crop failure was serious but it did not occur throughout Ireland. Real disaster struck in 1846. Captain Mann, a coastguard worker, wrote 'I shall never forget the change in one week in August. On the first occasion I had passed over thirty two miles thickly studded with potato fields in full bloom. The next time the face of the whole country was changed, the stalk remained bright green but the leaves were all scorched black. It was the work of a night.'

In 1846 the harvest was generally bad and poor people were at the end of their resources. Autumn turned into winter. Blackberries, nettles, rosehips, chickweed, hazelnuts and all other forms of free food disappeared.

Horror stories were reported. A woman and her two children were found dead on their farm at Caheragh, County Cork. Their bodies were half eaten by dogs. Nicholas Cummins, a Cork magistrate visited Skibbereen in December 1846. He was surprised to find the place apparently empty. He entered the first hovel to see what was happening and found six famished, ghastly skeletons lying on filthy straw. At first he thought they were dead but low moaning showed them to be alive, a man, a woman and four children. They had fever. Within minutes he was surrounded by 200 skeletal people. Later in the day he saw a mother, herself suffering from fever, drag the body of her young daughter out of her home and leave it half covered with stones. In another house he found seven wretched people, so weak they could not move, lying huddled under a cloak. One was dead, but the others could not move themselves, never mind move a corpse.

The climate in Ireland is usually mild. The winter of 1846-47 was 'the most severe in living memory' and the longest. It seemed as if Nature had joined Ireland's enemies. Snow fell early in November and was followed by continuous frost and icy gales.

Relief schemes were organised. They were very inefficient. On 24th October Denis McKennedy died while working on Road No.1, in the western division of West Carberry, County Cork. He had not been paid since 10th October. A post-mortem showed that he had died from starvation. There was no food in his stomach or in his small intestine. The large intestine was found to contain a 'portion of undigested raw cabbage mixed with excrement.' The inquest found that he had 'died of starvation caused by gross neglect of the Board of Works.'

Food, such as grain, was exported from Ireland during the famine.

The Government believed in free enterprise. It felt that food exported from Ireland could be sold at high prices and the money used to import cheap food for sale. This did not work because large numbers of people never bought food. They simply grew potatoes and ate them.

The more humane landlords organised soup kitchens to help their starving tenants. Eventually the Government developed the idea and organised soup for the starving. A lot of the soup was terrible. The Right Hon. James Grattan of Vicarstown, Queen's County had thirty gallons of soup distributed. The local school master described it as a 'vile compound' and the people, after one trial meal, refused to eat it because it gave them 'bowel complaints'.

There was no legal register of deaths during the period so the number of people who died is unknown.

More people died of 'famine fever' than of starvation. Bodies weakened by starvation are more prone to disease. People caught common diseases, such as dysentery, diptheria, scarlet fever, tuberculosis, influenza and so on and died from them. Typhus and relapsing fevers were also present. There were cholera epidemics in 1831, 1832 and 1848.

Starving, desperate people began running away from a country that appeared cursed. Tens of thousands fled across the sea. Unfortunately they brought disease with them.

As Ireland became depopulated the pressure for space decreased. There was no need to cultivate hilltop ground. To this day the outline of lazy beds, once used for cultivating potatoes, may be traced under the heather on hill tops such as Belfast's Cave Hill, Slieve Gullion in County Armagh and on the tops of the Glens of Antrim.

My great grandmother's maiden name was Martha Cooper. She died in Belfast in 1942 aged 84 years. She was the grand daughter of Sammy Cooper, the nailer. Sammy Cooper lived with his family in a house, with a small garden, in Antrim. She told my grandmother her mother remembered the Famine vividly. I do not know if she was referring to the Great Famine (1846-1847), or another period of famine.

Apparently, one of Sammy Cooper's jobs was to ring the Steeple bell each day so that the 'poor people' would know to come for their soup. Sometimes his wife rang the bell for him. He told her not to go near the 'poor people' because it could be dangerous. She could become diseased. She used to watch from a distance as ill-clad, starving wretches came and queued quietly for food. She wished she could help. She said if she had been starving she would have pushed her way to the front of the queue. These people stood quietly, in depressed lines.

Today, nearly one hundred and fifty years later, whenever I remember the sadness expressed by my grandmother when she talked about the famine, I feel rage that so many people starved to death. What could have been done to avert disaster? What is being done for starving people today in places such as Ethiopia? Are the developed nations, with the advantages provided by modern means of transport and modern medical knowledge, being any more successful in preventing people starving to death than the attempts made to help the Irish in the past?

Ruins of work house near Dunfanaghy, August 1989.

34

Chapter 5

EMIGRATION

Emigration did not come easily to the Irish as they loved their homeland. This love has survived through generations of emigrant families. It is impossible for any Irish person to visit the United States of America, Canada, the British Mainland, Australia or New Zealand without being told by numerous people 'My family originally came from Ireland'.

The emigration caused by the famine was of unskilled people into more skilled communities. The Irish poor had nothing to bring with them. They lived in the poorest of conditions in their new homes and were despised by other residents. Very few people who fled the famine became prosperous. It was not until the second and third generation that native Irish wit began to assert itself and the children and grandchildren of the poor famine emigrants became rich and powerful in their new lands.

During the early eighteenth century there was comparatively little emigration, mostly from Ulster, mainly Presbyterians of Scottish descent who wanted to better their lot. They were not paupers. They took money and experience with them.

The nineteenth century timber trade from British North America provided a way of escape. Ships came over loaded with timber. There was no demand for European goods in the New World so the ships had either to sail back carrying nothing but ballast or take passengers. Wooden berths were put up between decks and in the early days passengers had to bring their own food. The ship owners supplied fuel and water. Fares might seem low but the average family had to save for about one year in order to raise the money. It was possible to travel to Quebec for two or three pounds.

By 1845 carrying emigrants had reached the stage where larger profits were being made by the passenger trade than the timber

Replica Belfast Docks and Emigrant Ship, Ulster American Folk Park, Omagh.

trade. This was encouraged by the British Government because it allowed the timber to be sold at a low price.

Most Irish emigrants wanted to go to the United States of America. They went by a roundabout route. American ships were safer and better than British ones, but they were more expensive. In 1842 the fare from Belfast to Quebec was 6 pounds for a man, his wife and four children on a British ship. The fare to New York for the same family was 21 pounds. Most emigrants sailed to Quebec then crossed the border into the States.

As the winter of the famine 1846-47 dragged on, the snow fell and people became more and more desperate. Emigration continued across the Atlantic through the winter for the first time in history.

Conditions in Ireland were so awful that the Irish people became desperate to escape and were content to suffer great hardship during the voyage. They felt that they had nothing to lose, apart from their lives and their lives were in danger at home. Their desperation led to the existence of the 'coffin ships'.

'Coffin ships' were very old, overcrowded, and often short of legal quotas of food and water. They began to leave from smaller and smaller ports such as Ballina, Westport, Tralee and Killala.

Ships leaving from large ports such as Dublin, Belfast, Sligo and Waterford were comparatively well equipped.

The 'Elizabeth and Sarah' was a typical example of a 'coffin ship'. It sailed from Killala, County Mayo in July 1846 and arrived in Quebec in September. The Captain was incompetent so the passage took eight weeks, about twice as long as the normal duration of the voyage. The passenger list showed 212 names but the ship carried 276 people. She should have had 12,532 gallons of water, but had only 8,700 gallons stored in leaking casks. The Passenger Act of 1842 ordered 7lbs. of provisions to be given out each week to each passenger. No food was ever given out on the 'Elizabeth and Sarah'. The ship had 36 berths 4 of which were taken by the crew, 276 passengers shared the remaining 32 berths, or slept on the floor. There was no toilet of any kind on board so conditions within the vessel became disgusting. Passengers were starving and tortured by thirst, 42 of them died during the course of the voyage.

A 'coffin ship' sailing from Westport is said to have sunk within sight of land, watched by relatives and other loved ones, to whom the emigrants had just said 'Goodbye'. There was not a single survivor.

Officials in Canada were worried about the effect of the disease-ridden Irish on their country. They decided that all ships carrying

Emigrant Ship, Ulster American Folk Park, Omagh.

passengers up the St. Lawerence should stop at a quarantine station on Grosse Isle, thirty miles down the river. Vessels with sickness on board were to be detained and the sick taken off for treatment in the quarantine hospital. The medical officer in charge of the quarantine station, Dr. Douglas, asked on 19th February 1847 for 3,000 dollars to make preparation for the expected springtime immigration. He was given less than 300 dollars and allowed a small steamer to ply between Grosse Isle and Quebec. He was also given permission to hire a sailing vessel, provided he could do so for 50 dollars for the season.

During April the hospital became overcrowded so Dr. Douglas asked for permission to build a new shed for 150 dollars. He was granted 135 dollars. By 24th May all accommodation was dangerously overcrowded. There were 695 people in hospital and 164 on board ship waiting to land. On 26th May 30 vessels with 10,000 emigrants on board were waiting at Grosse Isle. By 31st May 40 vessels were waiting in a line extending 2 miles down the St. Lawrence. There were 1,100 cases of fever on Grosse Isle in tents, sheds, and laid out in rows in the little church with an equal number on board the ships waiting to be taken off. At least another 45,000 emigrants were expected.

The emigrants were in a terrible state when they landed. They tottered off the ships — feeble, spectre-like wretches who died in their thousands. Emigrants died, doctors and nurses died. Equipment in the hospitals was practically non-existent. Bedding had been sent down but there was nothing to put it on and it soon became soaked on the ground. Medical staff became unobtainable.

Over 100,000 emigrants left Ireland for British North America in 1847. It has been estimated that 20,000 died in Canada and at least 25,000 people had been in Canadian hospitals while 17,000 died during the voyage. One of the Commissioners for Emigration in the United States wrote 'If crosses and tombs could be erected on the water the whole route of the emigration vessels from Europe to America would have long since have assumed the appearance of a cemetery.'

Chapter 6

PIGS, HENS AND HORSES

Farmers who were so poor that they could not afford a cow probably had a pig and some hens. These animals were very important because they helped the farmer earn money to pay the rent. The family pig was often called 'the gentleman who pays the rent.'

Pigs are very like humans in many ways. Their skin has a poor covering of hair so they like heat. They appreciate being clean and can be house trained so pigs were often treated like family pets.

William Carlton wrote in 'Traits and Stories of The Irish Peasantry', about Phil Purcel the pig driver. He described the amazement of a visitor to Phil's father's homestead. They were sitting 'cracking' around the fire when an old pig came in through the door, walked over to a ladder that was leaning against the half loft, climbed it and settled down for a sleep. The father explained that the old pig was very wise and very clean. When it slept, as it often did, near the fire with the occupant of the outshot bed, it always stayed on the side of the bed away from the wall, so if it wanted to go to the toilet in the middle of the night it could get out without disturbing anyone. Apparently that pig had sired many fine piglets and Phil's father expressed the feeling that no-one had a greater right in the house than the gentleman who paid the rent.

Phil reared an ancient Irish type of pig that is now extinct. This old breed of pig was tall with long legs, short ears and a long intellectual looking face. It was called the 'greyhound pig' because of its slim appearance and long legs. It could jump over fences which were four feet in height. According to Phil it was impossible to fatten this type of pig, but it was very easily trained and could respond to instructions given to it in Irish and in English. Furthermore, if this type of pig had the opportunity of living with a hedge schoolmaster it could also learn to respond to orders given to it in Latin!

Don't forget — when you escape walk about one hundred yards behind me.

A pig that was house trained was referred to as an 'educated pig'. An educated pig was allowed to wander around the small holding during the day. It returned to the house at meal times and took its proper place sitting in the circle around the cooking pot at meals. The pig was placed beside the youngest children. Sometimes the educated pig and the young children squabbled over food.

Phil Purcell used to collect a herd of pigs, drive them to the boat and travel to the British mainland with them. The pigs, with their slim bodies and long legs, were very agile. Phil sold them to English farmers who thought they could make a profit on the deal by fattening the pigs with good food. Phil sold his pigs including one special pig that was particularly well educated. This pig was trained to jump fences and escape. Phil walked around the neighbourhood whistling. His special pig was trained to escape and walk about a hundred yards behind him. Once Phil was reunited with his special pig he moved onto the next town and sold it again! Anyone seeing Phil travelling from town to town simply saw a man walking by himself. It was unlikely that anyone would connect Phil with the pig wandering along the road some distance behind.

The Large White Ulster was another famous breed of local pig. It, as the name suggests, was very different from the slim, long legged animal bred by Phil Purcell. It was a big pig that put weight

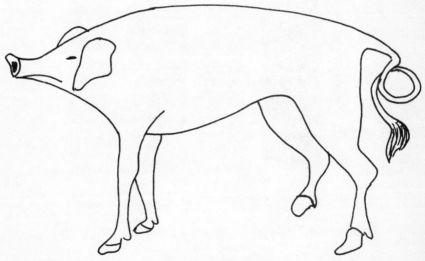

Irish Greyhound Pig.

41

Terrace house, East Bread Street, Newtownards Road, Belfast.

on easily. This was an advantage because the heavier the pig the more money it raised when it was sold. Many Large White Ulster pigs became so cumbersome that folds of fat covered their eyes and they became blind. The Large White Ulster is also extinct.

Pigs were raised and slaughtered on farms until the 1930s when the Pig Marketing Scheme was introduced. This scheme forbade the slaughtering of pigs at home. They had to be killed in the abbatoir. The Large White Pig had a very thin skin so it was often damaged on the way to the abbatoir. Damaged pigs did not fetch as much money as undamaged ones so the Large White Ulster became less popular. The final blow to its production came with a change of fashion. The so called 'Wiltshire cure' became popular and replaced traditional methods of curing pigs. The Large White Ulster was unsuitable for that type of cure because it was too fat. The breed declined in numbers until it became extinct.

The Industrial Revolution in Belfast attracted workers who had been raised on farms. They brought their old habits and farming skills to the city. They often raised pigs and hens in the back yards of their terrace houses. Practically all the houses in areas like the Newtownards Road in Belfast had a pig and a few hens in the back yard.

A typical factory worker would have lived in a street similar, to East Bread Street off the Newtownards Road, and worked in the shipyard belonging to Harland and Wolff. Pigs in backyards were common until the 1930s. Any man who kept a pig was called a 'pig man'. 'Pig men' asked people in the surrounding area to keep left over food and vegetable peelings for their pigs. Boys, known locally as 'skins boys', walked along the back entries behind the terrace houses and collected each households refuse to feed the areas pigs. This practice continued until the 1950s.

When I was a young child I lived with my parents in Orby Parade, off the Castlereagh Road. I remember my mother placing vegetable peelings, uneaten potatoes and other household refuse in a bucket that was kept in an outhouse. Each week a 'pig man', carrying a huge bucket, opened the outhouse door, removed my mother's bucket and emptied its contents into his. The 'pig man' walked around the neighbourhood with his trousers tucked into muddy, wellington boots. He looked incongrous in a surburban neighbourhood.

Before legislation forbade it pigs were slaughtered at home. A pig was usually killed by being struck on the forehead with something heavy such as a sledge hammer. Its throat was then cut and it was hung up to bleed. After that boiling water was poured over the skin and it was scraped to remove hairs.

Once the pig was slaughtered nothing was wasted. It provided bacon and ham, much of which was smoked for preservation. The liver, heart and trotters were also eaten. Pigs' intestines were used as sausage skins, blood was turned into black pudding and even the stomach was used, stuffed with bread and herbs, as a local version of haggis.

Meat on pigs' trotters was thought to be particularly tasty. There was a small butcher's shop at the bottom of the Albert Bridge Road in Belfast. It was owned by Hugh Gemmell, an amateur poet. He always had a verse pasted on his shop front advertising the excellance of the pigs' feet which he had for sale. Once, shortly after the Second World War, when the shop was being renovated and a corrugated, iron hoarding was placed in front of it, the following verse appeared on the hoarding:-

> 'Behind this iron curtain,
> Gemmell's can't be seen,
> But 'though his shop is hidden,
> His feet are still supreme.

Hens were very important to the farmer's wife because tradition decreed that she was allowed to keep any money she earned from them. This gave her a little independence. The value of forty hens was thought to be equal to that of one cow. Leghorns, Sussex and Irish bare neck hens were breeds commonly found. The Irish bare neck hen is particularly interesting. It has, as the name suggests, no feathers on its neck. When it perches in a tree, or a barn, it bears a passing resemblence to a vulture.

According to Ernest Scott, a local historian from Ballynure, horses were extremely important to farmers who had a surplus of produce they wanted to sell. The only means of taking food to market before motorcars and lorries became common was to use a horse and cart. Ernest remembers helping his father load a cart and leaving his home at 3 o'clock in the morning to travel to Belfast to the market. They arrived in Belfast before 7 o'clock and sold their goods at the

"Just think — I am worth forty hens."

market. They used to have their breakfast in the Irish Temperance League Cafe at the corner of May Street. Breakfast consisted of an 'Ulster Fry', fried bacon, egg, potato bread, soda bread and sometimes a fried pancake as well. The cafe was warm and cosy and appeared particularly welcoming on a cold, wet morning in the middle of winter. According to Ernest the Temperance League organised Cafes to keep men from drinking heavily in Public Houses. Men had a tradition of going on the 'tear'. This meant that they disappeared into the local Public House and stayed there for days, weeks, or even months. Mothers, sweethearts and wives were expected to go on living normally until they returned. This tradition of heavy drinking had a devastating effect on families.

Ernest remembers ploughing with Clydesdale horses on his father's farm in Ballynure during the 1920s. Most Irish farmers had smaller horses because they used their horses for pulling traps, and riding as well as providing power to work heavy machinery and working in the fields. Sturdy cross-bred cobs with distinctive 'skewball' brown and white markings were common on small farms before the tractor was invented. This type of horse is still popular with gypsies.

The characteristics of a good horse were described as follows:-

'Three traits of a bull, a bold walk, a strong neck and a hard forehead.
three traits of a fox, a light step, a look to the front and a glance to each side of the road,
three traits of a woman, a broad bosom, a slender waist and a short back,
three traits of a hare, a lively ear, a bright eye and a quick run against a hill.'

According to folk lore horses understand human speech. They are capable of bringing luck. If a mare drops her seventh foal outside in the open tradition suggests that the field should be searched for a four-leafed shamrock. This will keep its owner from being deceived by magicians.

Horses were thought to be able to see ghosts more easily than humans and to be sensitive to places where evil has occurred. They were thought not to willingly pass a place where a murder has taken place.

Some people had the ability to calm horses. Sullivan, who lived near Newmarket, County Cork around 1830 had a secret way of calming horses. He went into a stable with a wild horse, shut all doors and led a quiet, calm horse out after approximately 30 minutes. He travelled around the countryside calming horses for a guinea or two. He kept his method so secret that he did not even tell his son with the result that his skill died with him.

The ability to calm horses was not confined to men. Maire O'Beirn who lived in County Kerry is an example of a woman who possessed the skill.

Many famous horses have come from Ireland, such as Napoleon's famous white charger 'Marengo.' He was bred in County Wexford and bought by a Frenchman who presented him to the Emperor at a later date. Strangely enough the charger ridden by Wellington at the Battle of Waterloo also came from Ireland. It was bought at a fair at Cahirmee.

Chapter 7

MARKETS, FAIRS AND FAKING

The dates on which markets and fairs were held were very important to most people in the past. Masters and servants, men, women and children, apprentices and journeymen had the right to leave their work for the day to meet their friends and enjoy the fun of the fair.

Markets and fairs meant serious business for many families as they tried to sell the animals and crops on which their livelihood depended.

Towns which oiginally had a fair, or a market, have a wide main street,or a large square, where people could sell goods. Weavers sold linen. Rushes were tied into bundles and taken to fairs to be sold to flax-farmers who used them as ties for beets of flax. Ling, that is, blue blossomed heather, was pulled from the hill-tops, pulled out by the roots and trimmed to make besoms. A besom was a type of broom.

Farmers brought their animals and crops, their wives brought butter, hens and eggs to sell.

There have been tremendous changes in transport and marketing during the past fifty years. New forms of entertainment have taken the crowds off the streets. These changes have led to the death of most fairs and markets. Some fairs, such as the Puck Fair at Kilorglin in County Kerry, have survived the passage of time. Some weekly markets, such as the flea market held in Dublin on Saturdays, the weekly markets held in Newry on Thursdays, in Lisburn on Tuesdays, and so on, still survive.

The most ancient fairs are those celebrating the ancient god of the Harvest, Lugnasa. Through time the name Lugnasa Fair changed to Lammas Fair. Lammas Fairs are held sometime in August (Lunasa is the Gaelic word for August). Their original purpose was to ensure fertility. The Puck Fair at Kilorglin and the Auld Lammas Fair at

Auld Lammas Fair, Ballycastle, August 1989.

Ballycastle are surviving examples of this type of Fair.

The Puck Fair is unusual because each year a goat is chosen and crowned king. It is then put into a cage which is hung high above the Fair while the people below drink, trade, look at street entertainments, have their fortunes told and generally enjoy themselves. It is said that any young woman attending the fair will have a baby during the following year. My daughter was born during the Spring in the year after I visited the Puck Fair. I do not know if that is a coincidence or not!

The Auld Lammas Fair at Ballycastle is a slightly more sober occasion. It does not have the benefit of a goat crowned as king. The tradition is much more prosaic, one simply buys a sticky, hard, honeycomb toffee called 'yellow man' and eats dulse. Dulse is a type of seaweed. It is collected from the shores around Ireland, dried and eaten. In the days when hunger stalked the land, dulse was a useful additional food during the long days of summer, when foodstores were running low and the next harvest was not ready. It contains vitamins and mineral salts including iodine. It has a salty taste and makes people thirsty, so that they are inclined to drink

Banbridge Town. The wide street is a sign that in the past a market was held in the town.

Sign advertising the Boley Fair, Hilltown, July 1989.

more than usual. As in the Puck Fair, people go to trade, have their fortunes told and enjoy the buskers and other forms of street entertainment.

Banbridge, like many other country towns, had a street market. It was held on Mondays. Farm produce, flowers, linen, general goods and livestock were sold. The market gradually lost popularity over the years until the only person left was a street trader who sold plants on Mondays during the summer months. In addition to the weekly markets there were Horse Fairs.

Most of the old fairs and markets died when a good transport system developed which enabled farmers to sell goods far a-field. Some of the fairs turned into sites for Fun Fairs.

There has been a recent attempt to revive some of the old fairs as tourist attractions. Hilltown has revived its Boley Fair and Dromore, County Down again has an annual Horse Fair. It is interesting to see horses led up the street, showing their paces and people bargaining although I have not seen anyone seal a bargain in the way my mother described. The buyer and the seller spat on their own right hand. They then shook hands so that the spit on each hand was combined.

It was traditional, once the bargain was sealed and money had exchanged hands, for the buyer to return a piece of silver to the seller as a 'luck penny.'

Horses were an extremely important means of transport and remained so until the 1950s.

When I was a child, growing up in Belfast during the 1950s, pint bottles of milk were delivered to my house each day by a milkman who had a cart and a horse called 'Hamlet'. The milkman told me he was expected to take Hamlet to the stables each night and attend to its needs. He groomed the horse and fed it. He said he was expected to keep the area, in which the horse was stabled, clean.

The milkman grieved whenever Hamlet was replaced by a van sometime in the 1950s. Hamlet was replaced because it was much cheaper to buy petrol and maintain a van than it was to stable and look after a horse.

The milkman said his job became much more impersonal whenever his horse was replaced. Collecting a van was an entirely different think to collecting Hamlet each morning because Hamlet always appeared pleased to see him. Also, some people came out of their houses to talk to the horse. Nobody paid any attention to the van! Hamlet had his own friends, people who fed him tidbits such as lumps of sugar, bread or carrots. Hamlet learned where he received treats and set off down the street on his own to his favourite houses. The milkman said Hamlet's behaviour added interest to his round. My neighbours also missed Hamlet. They used to rush out quickly and pick up his droppings with a brush and shovel to put around their roses. The roses did not do so well once Hamlet had gone!

Many horses were employed in Belfast. Belfast once had horse drawn trams for public transport. Milk. coal and bread were delivered to householders using horse drawn transport. Many firms were involved. A city bakery, and there were many bakeries, would have needed about 100 horses in its stables to make sure that its product was distributed efficiently.

The horse was essential to farmers with sufficient land to produce a surplus. Horses were needed to prepare the land for growing crops, to help with the harvest and to take the produce to market.

Dealers hired gangs of men to bring horses to market. Each man rode on the bare back on one horse and led about six others, strung together by their halters. The men were usually rough and poorly clad, but were affable and jolly. They stayed with their charges and often slept beside them out on the streets.

Horses and donkeys would begin to arrive for a horse fair several days before the event. By the time the big day arrived the town concerned would be very congested.

People living in terrace houses along streets holding fairs had to go in and out through the back doors because their front doors would be blocked by livestock.

The Irish have a reputation for kindliness. Local inhabitants were often very good to the men tending animals. Robert Grange lived in Mill Lane, Ballyclare. He remembers how his mother used to take refreshments, such as a bowl of broth, a cup of tea, or a farl of soda bread, to the horse handler outside her door.

Dealers invited seemingly nonchalant buyers strolling up and down, to try out stock. The animals would be standing shoulder to shoulder in a line along the footpath. An animal would be chosen and raced up and down the road to show its shape and prowess. This practice, which is still common in horse fairs held today, is a trial of wind and limb. It also shows how an animal places its feet when it walks. This is crucial if the horse is intended for use in potato or turnip drills. A 'splay-footed' horse would make a mess of any drill.

Running horses among people is dangerous. Sometimes spectators were killed. The 'Belfast News Letter' for Wednesday 21st May 1879 describes how one man was killed when a horse kicked back and struck him on the upper portion of his body.

Charlie McCourt, an old age pensioner who lives in Banbridge, told me how as a boy he watched men faking horses in an entry off Dromore Street at 'the foot of the town.' The horses were sold later in the day at the market in the town. According to Charlie sickly animals were 'doctored' to look 'wonderful'. Old horses had their grey hairs dyed with Indian ink or touched up with boot polish to make them look younger.

It is possible to tell a horse's age from its teeth so some horses had their mouths doctored. The teeth at the back of the mouth were removed to make it look younger. Teeth were filed down and a fake black spot placed in the middle of each one also to give a younger appearance. If a horse's face was pathetic looking, with sunken eyes then the hollows were injected with water. The water filled the hollows and gave a nice rounded appearance.

Horses with broken wind were fed normal food mixed with lead shot to disguise the defect.

Lame horses were inspected very carefully. It required great expertise to make a lame horse appear normal! There were two methods of doing it. One was to remove the shoe from the good leg, the other was to kick the good leg hard. Both methods caused the animal to walk evenly. It depended on the individual horse which was the better method to use!

Bad tempered horses were fed dope to quieten them down so that they appeared gentle at sale time. The effect of the dope lasted a few days after which the horse reverted to type.

Skewbald horses, that is, horses with coats of two colours, were thought to be unlucky. They were often dyed so that they appeared to be one colour. There are many tales of people who bought a horse at a Fair and rode it through the rain. By the time they reached home the dye had washed off the animal and it looked very different from when it had been bought.

"Never mind what the horse feels like — I'll make it look better."

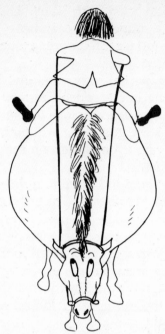

"Mummy! Mummy! Come quickly! Dobbin's rump has changed colour since we bought him yesterday."

Charlie also told me that an animal could be made to look a lot more lively by sticking a wad of tobacco up its backside. Apparently this treatment made it hold its tail out with spirit and move faster. He said he remembered one poor, old horse in particular. It came in with its head hanging down and its tail between its legs. It looked as if it could hardly place one foot past the other. After the tobacco treatment it was revived as if by magic and shot out of the yard like greased lightning with its tail well up!

Ginger was another substance used to stick up an animal's backside to make it appear livelier. Charlie said that all animals could be treated with tobacco, or ginger, to make them appear more lively. He saw horses, cows, sheep and pigs being treated in this manner.

There is a tale of a man from Ballymena who had a very slow sow for sale. The animal was so slow it could hardly move. He took it to the market at Ballymena, gave it the ginger treatment and sat beside it all day trying to sell it. He could find nobody foolish enough to buy the animal so, covered in despondency, he set off home. The animal staggered along in front of him, very, very slowly. Filled with impatience he tried kicking it to make it go a bit faster. The pig did not respond so he shoved some ginger up its backside. The animal ran so fast he could not keep up with it so in desperation he resorted to giving himself the ginger treatment!

Pork was sold in open markets until slaughter in abbatoirs became common. Farmers placed their pork in carts and joined a queue outside the Market House to have their carcases weighed. A farmer who did not receive a good price for his pork was in an impossible position. The meat decayed quickly in the days before refrigeration became available. A whole pig was difficult even a for large family to eat before it decayed.

A good market had a public weigh-bridge and a reliable operator. The Commissioners appointed to inquire into the state of fairs and markets in Ireland in 1853 uncovered a lot of dishonesty. Many of the weigh-bridges had two sets of weights, one for buying and one for selling. Other weigh-bridges had slides which allowed a bar of lead to be inserted so that a true weight was not obtained.

Farmers selling live animals, such as pigs, cows, sheep and horses could simply take their animals home again if they were not offered a reasonable price. They were then free to try and sell their animals on another occasion.

Fowl dealers visited markets regularly. They bought birds there. Some dealers also travelled around the countryside bargaining for birds at farm houses. They often travelled on bicycles with up to eight, half dead fowl tied to the handlebars.

Fowl were usually sold to dealers in bundles of five or six. Most bundles contained a dud or weakling along with good birds.

In the past hygiene was sadly lacking at markets and fairs, indeed it was lacking in shops as well. I remember an old shop on the Castlereagh Road in Belfast. It sold hardware and 'country butter'. The butter had a delicious flavour and so was much in demand. The shop and the old man who owned it were absolutely filthy, covered in grime. The place was extremely untidy, yet if one went in and asked for something small, say a pot mender, the owner would grunt, come out from behind the counter and begin fiddling among the untidy, dust-covered pile of goods which littered the shop floor. He invariably managed to find whatever was required within seconds. Believe it or not, the 'country' butter was concealed within the pile. It was produced with a flourish, banged upon the counter, unwrapped, the required amount cut from the slab, banged into shape by the man's dirty hands then wrapped in greaseproof paper. The butter was smuggled into Belfast from country areas and sold on the 'Black Market' during and for sometime after the Second World War when butter was rationed. My mother was a regular customer. She used to take the butter home, cut a thin slice off the outer edges and feed them to the cat. She thought the inside of the butter-pat, not touched by the shopkeeper's hands, was clean enough. She said dirty butter had a bad taste.

My grandmother showed me how to test butter. She said that a lot of the butter sold was rancid or over salted so it tasted awful. Housewives used to travel around the stalls and ask to taste the butter. The stall owners unwrapped the butter exposing the upper surface. The housewife took the nail of her forefinger and used it to scrape a little butter off the sample. If she liked the taste she asked for an amount, say a pound, to be cut off the slab. If she did not like the taste of the butter she refused to buy it.

Market Day.

56

Granny said she found it necessary to watch stall owners and make sure she obtained butter from the slab she had tasted and not from another slab in at the back of the stall. She had been very upset when, as a new bride, she had gone to buy butter at Belfast Market. She tasted it and it was good. The stall holder turned around very quickly holding the butter in her hands, as if she had been distracted by something, shouted across to another stall holder behind her, turned around again with butter still held in her hands and cut the required amount off. When granny took the butter home it was ghastly and she had to throw it out. She realised the stall holder had quickly changed slabs when she turned round.

Hiring Fairs were held on 1st May and 1st November. The days of the Hiring Fairs were traditional holidays so there was a great air of festivity. Young men and women made themselves a picnic lunch, packed their belongings into a parcel to tuck under their arms and set off to enjoy themselves. However, the day had a serious purpose. Before it ended they had to obtain a job for the next six months. Men and women seeking employment stood in the traditional places, men along one side of the street, women along the other and waited for potential employers to come and talk to them. They held their belongings proudly under their arms as a status symbol. It was important for the parcel to be large as that suggested prudence and comparative wealth due to the ability to earn a high wage. The parcels were often packed with straw to make them appear larger. Being interviewed at a hiring fair could be a humiliating experience. Potential employers were at liberty to ask very personal questions and to attempt to find out how strong individuals were by feeling their muscles.

I once met an old man in the doctor's surgery in Banbridge who said that fighting in the Second World War had been a horrendous experience. Nevertheless, he felt it had an overall helpful effect on his life. Before the war he had worked as a farm labourer, hiring himself out each May and November. He said he was quite sure there were good, generous people who provided good homes for their labourers. Unfortunately they were difficult to find. If an individual obtained a good home that person was very careful not to give offence and made sure that work was done in a pleasant, efficient way. As a result the majority of jobs were unofficially filled before the hiring fair. People in this happy situation simply went to the fair and struck up another agreement with their old bosses within the first five minutes, they then had the rest of the day off. There was a high level of unemployment so he, along with others in the same position, had to hang around, feeling humiliated and receiving unreasonable offers from miserly individuals. He escaped the system by signing up when the War started. He learnt a trade in the Army and came back after the war as a skilled labourer who never again had difficulty in obtaining employment.

The individual who had been hired was given a small amount of money, usually a silver shilling, to seal the deal. He, or she, was then entitled to 'free' board and lodging until the next Hiring Fair and a small wage. The wage, minus the shilling, became due at the

Things have changed: Shopping Centre, St. Stephen's Green, Dublin 1989.

Things have changed: Castle Court Shopping Centre, Belfast.

end of the period in question. If the hired individual became disgruntled and left employment, before the time was finished the contract was said to be null and void and no money was paid. Many dishonest farmers tried to make life impossible for their hired hands, towards the end of the period, in the hope that they would leave and be unable to obtain their wages.

Some hired hands were treated as members of the family, others were very badly treated, expected to sleep in the barn, have their frugal meals placed on the doorstep and to eat alone outside.

A way of life has gone and it would be sentimental to mourn its passing. Much of the filth and violence associated with animals, crowds and drink has also disappeared.

Chapter 8

BANSHEES, LEPRACHAUNS, FAIRIES AND GIANTS

In the past people tended to be very superstitious because, without the benefit of modern scientific knowledge, they lacked understanding about such things as the causes of disease, changes in the weather, decay and so on. Events that could not be explained were thought to be due to supernatural beings such as fairies. It was said to be impossible to see fairies without believing in them.

Irish folklore contains many references to different types of fairy. Fairies were referred to as 'the wee folk', or 'the good people.'

According to tradition there once was a great war in Heaven between God and the devil. The fairies took no part in the fight. They remained neutral throughout. The war ended when God managed to throw the devil into hell. God said to the Fairies 'You cannot stay in Heaven because you did not join with me in the fight against the devil, on the other hand it would be wrong for you to go to hell as you did not fight against Me.' He threw the fairies out of Heaven and some of them landed on the earth, others landed under the earth and some ended up in the sea. Fairies are believed to be immortal because they originally came from Heaven.

Elizabeth Andrews, in her book 'Ulster Folk Lore' suggests that a primitive, pigmy race existed in Ireland and that this race lived in the souterrains. Souterrains are underground chambers. That would explain why ordinary people claimed to have heard music coming from under the ground. An individual catching sight of a member of the pigmy race would believe a fairy had been sighted.

There is a genetic disease called achronoplastic dwarfism that is passed from one generation to the next. An achronoplastic dwarf is a perfectly normal individual who has shorter arms and legs than usual. The defect is obvious at birth. The dwarf will not grow any larger than the average six or seven year old child. In the past people had a very unsympathetic attitude to pain, suffering and misfortune. They believed these things were caused by wicked behaviour. As a result defective children were hidden because they gave rise to gossip. Friends and neighbours would wonder what sin the family had committed to deserve such a punishment. Even Queen Victoria was not immune. She kept her backward son hidden. At least some families with achronoplastic dwarf children would have kept them hidden. Perhaps an individual catching a glimpse of an achronoplastic dwarf would have believed that a fairy had been sighted. The dwarf's family would have had no wish to shatter the illusion.

My grandmother, Elizabeth Henry, died on 17th March 1951 aged 71 years. She was born in 1879. She had a very great friend called Maud Browne. Maud was an achronoplastic dwarf who had been brought up in an orphanage. She did not know anything about her parents. Apparently she had been found as a newborn baby beside a rath. Maud said that she was told that she had been left out for the fairies to claim as their own but she was not a fairy, just a perfectly normal being, trapped inside an odd-looking body. If she had been hidden rather than abandoned she might have been mistaken for a fairy.

It was thought unlucky to build a house on the site of a rath or

The Fairy Mountain, Tieverragh, Cushendall, County Antrim.

Don't look now Maisie, but there's something worse than a banshee behind us.

on the side of a fairy hill, such as that near Cushendall. Nobody should interfere with a fairy thorn. There are many tales around the countryside of people interfering with fairy thorns and suffering misfortune as a consequence. One of the most interesting is about the British Enkalon factory at Antrim. Apparently there was a fairy thorn on the site. It held up development of the factory as it was impossible to find anybody who would uproot it. Eventually a man came forward, said he did not believe in fairies and all that nonsense. He removed the thorn with a bulldozer. Later in the day the bulldozer fell into a hole in the ground in the field that had held the fairy thorn and the man was injured.

Banshees are the most misunderstood fairies in Ireland. They are softhearted, harmless creatures yet their appearance gives rise to the most profound fear. Banshees are female, with an awesome appearance. They are usually very beautiful with pale faces and long, flowing, dark hair.

Only members of the old families in Ireland have banshees attached. The banshee appears to warn of an imminent danger of death. If a person is about to die it is useful to know so that affairs may be put into order, old grievances settled and so on. The banshee does not cause death, simply warns that it is likely. Banshees are softhearted. They are very upset at the idea of a death. That is why they sit and cry whenever they appear. If a crowd of banshees appears and starts singing and clapping their hands that means someone very important is about to die.

There was an old lady whose family name was Cassidy. She lived near Melmore Head in County Donegal. She said she saw crowds of banshees wailing for six nights before the First World War was declared and that the same thing happened before the declaration of the Second World War.

The current President of Ards Historical Association, a retired doctor, told me that about fifty years ago he visited a patient, who was a retired schoolmistress. She lived on the Ards peninsula and she was very upset. The previous day she had received a letter from her brother, who lived in America, saying he intended to come home to Ireland on a visit. That night the 'family's little lady' appeared on the wall outside her bedroom window, weeping and wailing throughout the night. The doctor was still with his patient when a telegram boy appeared with a telegram from the States. It told

63

her that her brother had had a very serious heart attack and was not expected to live. The brother did recover and was able to visit his sister at a later date.

The doctor originally came from County Tyrone. He told me when he was a boy he was acquainted with a family who had a daughter who had emigrated to America. The daughter became very upset because the family banshee appeared to her. She wired home to ask if anything was wrong and received a wire saying that her father had died on the day the banshee appeared.

According to tradition there is a banshee associated with the O'Neill family in Shane's Castle. There is a face in the wall of the castle. This face has the features of the family banshee. When the banshee appears with her warning the features of the stone face become more pronounced.

Leprachauns are another type of fairy. They are shoemakers. They dress in green and have large, black hats with a buckle at the front. In times of trouble they watch where people hide their gold so they know where to find it. There is always gold at the end of a rainbow! Fairies must always obey humans so anyone lucky enough to catch a leprachaun may demand a crock of gold. Leprachauns do not like parting with their treasure and are very cunning. They usually

O'Hare's Bar, Carlingford.

manage to trick the human into letting them go free, leaving their stores of gold intact.

A publican in Carlingford has a suit of leprachaun clothes and some bones displayed in his bar. He says they were brought in by a man who found them in the mountains behind the village. Many people appear to take this very seriously. The tourist board organises leprachaun hunts each spring. A crock of gold is hidden in the mountains and licences are sold enabling individuals to search for the gold and keep anything found. The bar is in the main street of Carlingford and belongs to P. J. O'Hare.

The cluricaun is an odd sort of fairy. It, like the leprachaun, is solitary and dresses with unfairylike homeliness. Cluricauns are very rare, especially in the North of Ireland. They spend their time drinking and becoming drunk in gentlemens' cellars. Some people argue that cluricauns do not exist as a separate entity. They believe cluricauns are simply leprachauns with bad habits.

The Fear Dearg, or Red Man, is also like a leprachaun. He wears a red coat and a red hat and spends his life playing practical jokes. Unfortunately Red Men possess a rather macabre sense of humour so their practical jokes are usually gruesome and nasty.

Fairy mistresses, called Leanhaun Shee are also thought to exist. Leanhaun Shee are very beautiful They fall in love with mortal men and tempt them to make love. If the man consents, he becomes enslaved and cannot escape, unless he finds another victim to replace him in his mistress's affections. If he cannot he is doomed. He will sicken and die. He cannot obtain peace. In the afterlife he is condemned to wander the earth for ever as a ghost. On the other hand, if he manages to resist the charms of the Leanhaun Shee she becomes enslaved to him. Leanhaun Shees often inspire their victims to write great poetry. Tradition suggests that is why many of the poets in Ireland died young.

The common, or garden fairies, are dainty individuals with wings. They, like the other types, are thought to live in fairy forts or raths and to leave changelings in place of humans. In the past the nature of disease was not understood. The onset of serious disease may change the appearance so it is logical to suggest sick people were mistaken for changelings. This was unfortunate because of the belief that changelings would disappear if burnt and the stolen individual would then be returned. There is a story about a man who thought

Rock structure, Giant's Causeway, County Antrim.

Finn McCool's boot, Giant's Causeway, County Antrim.

a changeling had been left in the place of his dearly loved wife. He picked his wife up and threw her on the fire. She burnt to death. The man was overcome with sorrow and committed suicide. Black (typhus) fever changed the appearance of its victims to such an extent that their relatives did not recognise them. It is very likely that a few black fever victims were suspected of being changelings and burnt to death.

Mothers were advised never to leave a baby sleeping alone beside the fire without leaving the fire irons across the cradle. Iron was thought to offer protection against fairies.

What happened to the fairies? Belief in them is not as common as in the past. Some say that fairies have left Ireland. There are many explanations offered for their disappearance. Some say they became disgusted by human behaviour and went into the walls at Killyleagh, others say the fairies from the North of Ireland fought those from the South and they annihilated each other. Another explanation is that they blew away in the 'big wind' of 1839, a horrendous wind that caused widespread damage throughout Ireland.

Ireland also possesses legends about giants. Finn McCool is one of the most famous giants. He is supposed to have had a bad temper and a hatred for the giant who lived in Scotland. According to folklore he lost his temper one day with the giant in Scotland, bent down and picked up a handful of earth to throw at his enemy. He missed, the earth fell into the sea and formed the Isle of Man while the hole left behind filled up with water and turned into Lough Neagh, the largest inland water in the British Isles.

The Giant's Causeway on the North Antrim coast is also said to be the result of Finn McCool's activities. Legend suggests he started to build the causeway out into the sea so that he could cross over and kill the giant who lived in Scotland. Finn died before the causeway was finished. He left one of his boots behind and that has turned to stone.

In Ireland today few people admit to believing in fairies, leprachauns or giants. However, many people are fearful of the supernatural. The type of feelings commonly expressed are — 'I do not believe in fairies, but I will not interfere with that fairy thorn just in case it could cause trouble!'

Chapter 9

CURES AND CUSTOMS

Life must have been very frightening in the past because people did not have the benefit of modern, scientific knowledge. Animals, people and crops could suddenly sicken and die without apparent reason. The all important weather could turn nasty and destroy a crop.

In the past people lived very much closer to nature than they do today. They were constantly on the lookout for signs that could be used to foretell the future. This gave rise to superstition and to ideas, based on observation, that were useful. Superstitions, ideas and oberservations from the past are preserved in folklore.

> 'Red sky at night
> Shepherd's delight.
> Red sky in the morning
> Shepherd's warning.'

In Ireland it is amazing how frequently good weather follows an evening during which the sky was red and how frequently a day of bad weather is preceeded by a red sky in the morning.

People used to take careful note of the first butterfly they spotted in the year. A brown butterfly was said to mean that the individual would eat brown bread for the remainder of the year. Brown bread was eaten by people who were not wealthy so the brown butterfly was a sign of poor crops and poverty. On the other hand a white butterfly denoted white bread and wealth. People in Ireland today are becoming increasingly health conscious so that attitudes to brown and white bread have changed. Brown bread, on account of its higher fibre content, is believed to be better than white.

Butterflies hatch at different times of the year, depending on temperature, so it could very well be that when the conditions cause white butterflies to hatch first they will also be good for growing crops. Butterflies were thought to be the souls of the dead.

There is a story of a little girl whose grandfather had just died. A butterfly flew into the house and she chased after it. Her grandmother was very cross and scolded her saying that she should let her grandfather rest in peace. The little girl cried for the rest of the day because she loved her grandfather and was upset to think that she had disturbed him.

There is an old saying regarding magpies:-

'One for sorrow
Two for joy.'

Fishermen used to look carefully for magpies. If the weather is going to be poor, one magpie from each breeding pair remains on the nest while the other forages for food, so the old rhyme is based on observation. In the past people thought that the bad luck foretold by the sight of a solitary magpie could be averted by greeting it with the words: 'Goodmorning Mr. Magpie.'

When the rooks build their nests high in the trees that is a sign of a good summer. Frogs lay their eggs in the centre of the pond, if the weather is going to be warm, and at the edge, if it is going to be cold. A plentiful supply of hawthorne and rose hip berries in autumn means that the winter is going to be very cold.

There is an old saying about bees:-

'A swarm of bees in May
Is worth a load of hay.
A swarm of bees in June
Is worth a silver spoon.
A swarm of bees in July
Is not worth a fly.'

In other words, if the weather is sufficiently good to enable bees to pollinate plants early in the year and then to reproduce and swarm the harvest will be good. If the bees are not able to swarm until later in the year then the crops will be poor.

Old folk cures are also interesting. In the days before penicillin was discovered a piece of mouldy bread was always kept in a safe place. Penicillin is a very common mould as Sir Alexander Fleming found in 1928 during the time in which he worked in St. Mary's

We couldn't possibly be drunk — our heads are bound with ivy.

Hospital, London. Penicillin grows on mouldy bread. In the past mouldy bread was wrapped around cuts and subturating sores. The ancient Chinese wrapped sores on their feet in mouldy bread.

There is a story about a young boy who went to work in a cobbler's shop as an apprentice. He was asked to tidy the shop as his first job and left alone. The boy brushed the floor then spied all the cobwebs hanging from the ceiling. He thought they looked very dirty so used the brush to knock them down and to sweep gently around the ceiling. When the cobler returned he flew into a rage and beat the boy around the head for being so stupid. The cobwebs were used to staunch bleeding. They were wrapped around any cut the cobbler might happen to inflict upon himself with his sharp instruments. He told the unfortunate boy he would be held directly responsible if anyone on the premises bled to death before the spiders had time to renew their webs. Needless to say the boy never touched another spider's web.

Ivy was used as a cure for corns. It was tied around corns and left on for several days. Some people used to boil ivy leaves in water then use the water to wash the corns before rubbing them with the leaves.

People believed that if they bound their heads in ivy they could drink as much alcohol as they wanted without becoming drunk!

Pains caused by rheumatism were cured by being rubbed with garlic which was also thought good for colds and coughs. Garlic was also believed to be good for the blood and for heart complaints. Today doctors have discovered that garlic keeps blood from clotting too quickly and it reduces cholesterol levels.

Garlic was used for skin complaints. A cat, called Jason, lived in the Folk and Transport Museum at Cultra. Jason was pampered by the shop assistants and some of the attendants at the Museum. He had a tendency to develop skin complaints. He was taken to the vet on many occasions and received many expensive injections. In spite of all the care and attention lavished upon him his skin continued to be troublesome. Then one day someone decided to try the old folk cure, garlic on Jason's sores. Capsules of garlic were obtained. A capsule was punctured and its contents were squeezed over Jason's sores three times each day. They healed rapidly.

Garlic was a very common crop in Ireland until about the time of the First World War. It was used as a general 'cure all'. Slices of garlic placed in the shoes against the soles of the feet was a cure for whooping cough. This sounds ludicrous but it is a fact that garlic placed against the soles of the feet is smelt on the breath within fifteen minutes.

Feverfew was used to cure pain caused by rheumatism and headaches. Two or three leaves from the plant were placed inside a sandwhich each day and eaten. Modern research has shown that feverfew is an effective treatment.*

Digitalis, the drug found in foxgloves, is an old cure for heart disease that is still in use today. Foxgloves are very poisonous so they must never be eaten without supervision by a doctor.

*Johnston, Dr E.S. et al., 'Efficacy of Feverfew as Prophylactic Treatment of Migraine', The British Medical Journal, vol. 291 (31 August 1985).

Heptinstall, Dr S. et al., 'Extracts of Feverfew Inhibit Granule Secretion in Blood Platelets and Polymorphonuclear Leucocytes', the Lancet (11 May 1985).

Country cures act more slowly but have fewer side effects than modern medicines.

In the past many people were thought to have the ability to charm disease away. There was an old lady who lived at Aghalee who was said to have a charm for shingles. She is now dead. A friend described a visit to her. She gave him a flannel belt, with herbs inside, to wear next his skin, made the sign of the Cross over his head and muttered something strange about him. She refused any payment saying that the ability to cure came from God and could not be exchanged for money. Payment would cause her powers to disappear. My friend was very impressed and came home feeling he was bound to be better soon. Unfortunately he has a sensitive skin and the flannel irritated it causing him to itch. He removed the belt saying he would just let the shingles run their natural course! The cure was just as bad as the disease!

Betty Quinn, a local songwriter, is 76 years of age. Several years ago she burnt her right leg against an electric fire. The burn never healed properly and caused her a lot of discomfort. It appeared swollen, red and sore. Doctors seemed unable to prescribe anything to help. Eventually Betty heard of an old woman who lived near Coalisland and who was said to have a cure for 'bad legs.' Betty went to see her. The old woman invited her in and sat and chatted for some time. Eventually she said 'I think I can do something for your leg.' She made the sign of the Cross over Betty's head, then made other strange signs around about her, muttered something incomprehensible, said a prayer and Betty's leg felt a lot better. The swelling disappeared and the red mark faded.

Charms were handed down from one generation to the next and there is no doubt that some, at least, were effective. Many probably had the same type of effect as doctors have found today with their placebos.

Throughout Ireland there are places such as the Strule Wells near Downpatrick and the stream beside Saint Briget's Shrine at Faughart near Dundalk, which are believed to have curative powers.

The Strule Wells have many interesting legends explaining how they obtained their curative powers. One story suggests that Saint Patrick slept in a cave with his head resting against a rock and spring water sprayed his beard and clothes. Ordinary mortals would doubtless have cursed the water but Patrick was a Saint so he blessed it, giving it curative powers.

The stream associated with Saint Bridget's Shrine at Faughart is interesting. It comes rushing down the mountainside and different parts of it are associated with different parts of the body. People visiting the stream seeking a cure are expected to leave some sort of belonging behind. The general feeling is if one expects to take something away, in the form of a cure, some sort of symbol should be left in return. Stockings, handkerchiefs, socks and other small items of clothing, belonging to the pilgrims, are tied onto sticks, or anything else that is suitable, and left fluttering in the breeze.

The holy places associated with cures are not visited as frequently as they were in the past but some people still go.

It would appear many of the old folk cures are useful. They are not as strong as modern drugs but usually have fewer side effects but they take a longer time to work. There is an increasing interest in them and many are gaining a place in conjuction with modern medicine.

Pieces of cloth left by pilgrims hoping for a cure near St. Bridget's Shrine, Faughat.

Chapter 10
CALENDAR CUSTOMS

Each year the earth grows cold and plants stop growing. Deciduous trees lose their leaves and herbaceous plants appear dead. Then gradually winter turns into Spring and life appears renewed. Primitive people did not have the knowledge to understand the seasons. Each autumn they felt that perhaps the sun had disappeared for good. This belief led to superstitions and customs, some of which persist to the present day, incorporated in our Christian Festivals such as Christmas and Easter.

To begin with, evergreen plants were looked upon as something very special, they could survive the winter without losing their leaves. They never appeared dead so they came to symbolise everlasting life and were used as decorations at the ancient pagan festivals. Their presence demonstrated that winter does not necessarily result in death, the sun would return in the Spring bringing light, warmth and growth. When Jesus 'The Light of the World' was born His birthday came to be associated with the pagan feasts of the winter solstice. Pagan people found it easier to go on celebrating on the same day as they had always done — so the pagan feast became Christmas.

Christmas

The eastern church believed that Jesus was born on the 6th of January so they celebrated Christmas at a different time from the western church. During the fifth century all the churches, except the Armenian church, decided to extend the festivities until the 6th of January so that the celebration would also honour the baptism of Christ and the visit of the Three Wise Men. This is the origin of the twelve days of Christmas. In Ireland, even two generations ago, only the rich gave each other Christmas presents. Country

Lane Ballybracken, County Antrim. The seasonal changes shown by deciduous trees such as these, and other plants, led to fertility rites.

people would have expected a 'Christmas box' from their grocer. The box would have held food and perhaps a calendar.

The decoration of houses with holly and ivy as a symbol of everlasting life is a custom that survives from the past, so is the lighting of the Christmas, or Yule, Candle on Christmas Eve. A Yule candle was placed in the window as a symbol of hospitality to remember the circumstances of Christ's birth. The door of the house might be left open for the same reason. Yule candles were often coloured and each district appeared to have its own taste in colour. At the present time people tend to leave their curtains open at Christmas so that the light from their living rooms shines out. Christmas trees, with electric, fairy lights replacing candles, are commonplace.

Christmas Day was marked by Church services and by special meals. Many a poor family had their only meat dish of the year on Christmas Day. There is an old saying in County Down: 'Glory be to Christmas, the day we get the beef.' In actual fact the 'beef' was usually goose. Traditionally animals were also given extra food on Christmas day.

The Mummers

In Ireland the big event of midwinter was the visit of the mummers. It has been suggested that mumming came from a spring ceremony of Graeco-Oriental pagan origin and that the strength of feeling in Ireland about Christmas caused the custom to be moved from Spring to midwinter.

Mummers were a group of between eight and sixteen young men. They went from house to house performing a play based on an ancient fertility rite, in which death and coming back from the dead, symbolised the death of life in winter and the rebirth that happens every spring.

The mummer's play began with the actors' entrance. This was followed by some sort of fight between the two principal characters, usually St. Patrick and St. George, resulting in the death of one

I wonder what I should give Daisy to eat for Christmas?

77

Mummers.

of them. Many of the plays had a Turk in them because Turks fought the Crusaders. The play came to an end when a doctor revived the warrior who had been killed. This was followed by a number of colourful characters such as clowns, dancers and musicians whose main job was to collect money. Devil Doubt was a great favourite. He had a sweeping brush and a hat to collect the money:

> 'Here I am, little Devil Doubt
> If yous don't give me money
> I'll sweep yous all out!'

The Mummers usually wore long, white shirts decorated with coloured ribbons to make them look feathered. Some of the characters had their faces blackened, others carried cudgels, or swords and shields made of wood. Some characters wore tall hats made of paper or straw.

Mummers were territorial. If they met another group working on their territory they fought until one group became exhausted and retired. The other group continued mumming.

78

The Armagh Rhymers are, at the present time, the best known group of mummers. They make frequent appearances at the Ulster Folk and Transport Museum. One of the Armagh Rhymers, Dara Vallely, says that the plays frequently have a curative effect on people who are mentally disturbed. He described visiting Gilford in County Down. A young autistic boy was a member of the audience. The boy was completely withdrawn and never spoke. He became very excited by the noise and the colour of the play. He began talking to his teacher and members of his class. He went home and astonished his mother by saying, 'Mum, will you give me a banana?'

Hunting the Wren

The hunting of the wren on 26th December may also have come from Graeco-Oriental pagan customs. Bands of youths hunted for a wren and killed it. They dressed as fools, or as women, or in suits made from straw with straw masks. The youths formed a noisy procession and demanded money to bury the wren. The bird was carried on a decorated wooden tray, or on a holly bush. In more recent times a toy bird was used instead of a dead one and sometimes a bird was not used at all.

An interesting reason for killing wrens is suggested by Irish folk lore. Apparently Irish soldiers decided to mount a surprise attack on Cromwell and his army. Under the cover of darkness they managed to draw near to Cromwell and had nearly surrounded him when wrens, perched on the drums of Cromwell's troups, pecked at them with their beaks. They made such a noise that Cromwell and his army awoke, fell upon the Irish and slaughtered them. Wrens are killed on St. Stephen's Day, that is, December 26th, as revenge.

The Wrenboys might also perform a mummers play. The leader, carrying the dead wren in its hollybush, called for space to act the play:

> 'Room, room brave gallant boys
> Come give us room to rhyme
> We've come to show activity
> Upon this Christmas time
> Acts of young and acts of age
> The like was never acted on the stage

If you don't believe what I say
Enter in Sir Patrick and clear the way'

The Armagh Rhymers replace the dead wren with a brown potato!

New Year's Day

New Year's Day was a time for preserving the luck of the household. There was a belief that happiness and prosperity depended on the first person to enter the house on New Year's Day. A dark haired man was thought to be lucky as a first footer. Women were thought to be unlucky, especially if they had red hair. Marie Ward, who lives near Dromore, County Down, has described how her father made wisps from part of the last sheaf cut at the harvest. The stalks of the grain were plaited leaving the grain heads hanging. The stalk ends were held in place by brightly coloured ribbons tied into a bow. Every New Year's Eve, Marie's father sent her to Belfast with a wisp to his sister's house in one of the streets off the Lisburn Road. Marie had to find a dark haired man to carry the wisp and a lump of coal into the house before she could enter.

There is a tradition in some streets in Belfast which continues to the present day. According to Lil McCusken, who used to live in East Belfast, at midnight on New Year's Eve all the doors in the street open and people shout greetings, offer each other drinks and a neighbour walks a donkey around the houses. A donkey has a mark on its back that resembles a cross. Tradition says that Jesus put that mark there after riding on a donkey on Palm Sunday. The cross gives protection against evil. Lil has recently moved to the Lisburn Road area and says she misses the 'crack' on New Year's Eve because people in her new neighbourhood do not carry on the old custom. She says it is still present in her old street.

St. Bridget's Day

Traditionally in rural Ireland St. Bridget's Day was looked upon as the first day of spring. The saint was supposed to have placed her foot in the water on her feast day and caused the weather to begin to become warm.

Saints are commonly believed to return to earth for their festive day so the door was left on the latch so that the house could be entered easily.

St. Bridget's Shrine, Faughat.

In some districts dandelions are called St. Bridget's flower because they are usually the first flower to appear after her feast day.

St Bridget's Eve is the last day in January. On this day children pulled rushes (they were never cut) and usually left them outside the house. A special meal was prepared, usually consisting of pancakes or currant bread. Then a ceremony followed. This varied considerably from one neighbourhood to another. In some places a member of the family, usually a daughter, was sent out to represent the saint. She returned with the rushes and was made welcome. The family used the rushes to make St. Bridget crosses. In other places the crosses were made before the meal, sprinkled with holy water and placed under each dish. Once the crosses were made they were blessed either by the local priest, or by being sprinkled with Holy Water, or by being taken to Mass. They were then placed over the door, usually by the third day after the feast, in the hope that the family would have a plentiful supply of food for the following twelve months.

Sometimes St Bridget crosses were also placed under the thatch, or in the byre, to protect the house and livestock from fire and disease.

St Patrick's Day

St Patrick's Day has a curious lack of traditional customs although patriotic Irish wear a shamrock. St. Bridget encouraged the weather to become warmer, but it was St. Patrick who 'turned the warm side of the stone uppermost.' Farmers still like to have their potato crop in the ground before St. Patrick's Day.

The great 'moveable' religious festivals of the Church, Shrove, Easter and Whitsun, come after St. Patrick's Day. Their dates are determined by the day on which Easter falls.

Shrove Tuesday

Shrove Tuesday was never one of the great festivals in Ireland. Shrove Tuesday is the last day before the beginning of Lent so it was looked upon as a 'great day for weddings.' Weddings were forbidden during Lent. Lent is traditionally a time of self sacrifice. Today people still 'give up' things, such as chocolates, alcohol, smoking and meat for Lent. Shrove Tuesday is a day when it is customary to have a few treats, to indulge the body, before suffering the sacrifices made during the period of Lent. Pancakes are still made as a treat on Shrove Tuesday.

St. Patrick's Grave, Downpatrick.

Shrove Tuesday was thought to be a good day for playing tricks on children, courting couples and unmarried people. Children could be sent to a neighbour's house to ask for the loan of a 'pancake sieve,' and might innocently visit several houses before discovering the trick. They could also be sent next door to ask for 'the oil of a hazel,' that is, a good beating.

Easter

Easter begins on Good Friday because that is the day of the Crucifixion. In Ireland it was thought to be the luckiest day to begin sowing corn although ploughing and the use of iron implements were avoided.

Easter Sunday marked the end of Lent, a period of abstinence and self-denial. There was a gay atmosphere. In Ireland it was customary to wear an item of new clothing on Easter Sunday. As a child my sister and I always had a new summer outfit to wear to church on Easter Sunday. There were times when we stood shivering in our new, flimsy clothing during cold March gales. When we asked our mother why we could not be sensible and wear our old, winter coats she replied that she did not really know. She supposed it would be unlucky to do so. I remember one particularly cold Easter when my sister and I felt we would be lucky not to catch pneumonia!

Another old custom was to get up early in the morning to 'see the sun dance.' Tradition says that Christ rose from the dead at dawn on Easter Sunday and that the sun danced for joy. In remembrance the light from the sun was reflected on a silver spoon and allowed to dance on the wall. Sometimes a saucer of water was used instead. My grandfather used to get up early on Easter Sunday to watch the sun dance. He used a saucer of water and when he saw my amazement at the reflections dancing on the wall he took out his silver hunter's watch and swung it from its chain so that its reflection also danced on the wall. When I laughed and laughed he told me to remember that it was just an old fashioned custom with a serious thought behind it. He also said that no matter how dull and wet the weather was on Easter morning it was always possible to obtain a reflection of the dancing sun upon the wall.

In pagan times an egg was looked upon as an emblem of fertility, a symbol of the renewal of life. The early Christian Church used eggs as a symbol of the Resurrection. Traditionally eggs were eaten at Easter. In more recent times it would appear that chocolate eggs are eaten on Easter Sunday and hard boiled ones on Easter Monday.

Children rolled hard boiled eggs along the grass until they broke. Then they ate them. The hard boiled eggs were usually brightly coloured by being boiled with a dye. Sometimes patterns were made on the shells. The egg may have been wrapped in a piece of another plant, such as an onion skin, so that the part that was covered remained white. Sometimes the child's initials were rubbed on the egg with a tallow candle. The dye did not have any effect on the place where the tallow had been. The shells were often saved to decorate the May bush in the May Day festivities.

My mother remembered as a child going to Bellevue, which was then on the outskirts of Belfast, on Easter Monday and rolling her egg down the hill. Her father told her to roll her egg down hill as the Cross stood on the top of a hill. Mother's egg was dyed by boiling it in a pot with tea leaves. Sometimes the family gathered whin flowers and boiled the eggs with them and a teaspoonful of salt. Tea gave a brown dye while whin turned eggs yellow.

Whitsun

Whitsun is the seventh Sunday after Easter. It marks the coming of the Holy Spirit and the end of the Easter season. Strangely, in Ireland, it was thought to be a very unlucky day. People born on Whitsun were thought likely to have the evil eye, or to be fated to grow up and commit murder. A chicken was sometimes killed in the hands of a Whitsun child to serve as a substitute for a human life thus preventing the murder.

Fairies and evil spirits were thought to be around at Whitsun so people were advised not to fall asleep outside in case they were stolen. People were also advised not to cross water or to go to sea because the souls of those who had drowned would attempt to run away with anyone who went near them. Whitsun does not appear to have had associations with evil in Britain and it is difficult to say why it should do so in Ireland, especially as the coming of the Holy Ghost was a joyful Christian event.

May Day, the Festival of Beltaine

The gaelic name for the month of May is Beltaine. The festival of Beltaine was celebrated on the first of May. This was the first day of summer and a holiday. The crops were safely in the ground and people had a brief break before turf cutting and haymaking began. May Day was a day of gatherings and of fairs. A dish of stirabout (porridge) was always served on that day because it showed that the woman of the house was a good, thrifty housewife. She had made her corn last. Even those who were short of corn tried to save some for May Day.

Beltaine is one of the few pagan festivals that has not been absorbed into the Christian calendar. Fairies and witches were believed to have great power for evil on that day. Fairies were supposed to travel in groups from place to place, holding feasts and dances in raths. (Raths were made by prehistoric man. They were raised areas used as defensive positions for houses or as places where cattle would be safe.) Sometimes fairies wanted human company so they stole adults and children. Changelings were left in their place. A changeling was a fairy who took the place of a human.

Fairies were also thought to contaminate food on May Eve. They stole the real food away at night and left poisonous pieces of turf disguised to look like food behind. Any food left over from May Eve was not eaten. It was buried in the garden or thrown over the townland's boundary for the dogs.

Bonfires were lit, usually on the top of hills and men and women jumped over the flames and later drove their cattle through the smouldering ashes as protection against evil.

Milk cows were thought to be in need of special protection against evil. Bunches of primroses were tied to cows' tails because evil spirits were thought to be unable to touch anything guarded by them. Rowan trees were also thought to protect against evil so sprigs of rowan were hung outside the byre door, or placed on the milking vessel or hung from the cow's horns.

Witches had the power, especially at Beltaine, to turn themselves into hares. They could then suck milk from the cows and charm a year's supply of butter away. Witches also gathered dew on May Day by lifting it into a bucket or sheet from several fields. This cast a spell so that the milk belonged to the witch rather than the farmer.

The fire symbolises the heart of the house. On May Day witches were thought to be anxious to steal fire. As a result a number of

Guess why I have primroses tied on to my tail!

customs arose. In some places it was thought to be unlucky to kindle a fire on May Day. In other places it was considered unlucky to be the first house to show smoke, so on May morning the cattle were milked and the byre swept clean before the fire was lit. In other areas nobody lit a fire until smoke was seen rising from the priest's chimney.

In the past the manure heap was regarded as an inportant symbol of fertility. Rowan branches were placed on the manure heap to protect it from evil. In the days before artificial fertilisers the manure heap was vital to ensure the growth of crops so it was sensible to protect it against evil. Sometimes whin bushes were placed on the manure heap instead of rowan.

People collected flowers and scattered them along window sills, on door thresholds and sometimes on house roofs. My next door neighbour, who is eighty eight years of age, remembers that, as a girl living in Banbridge, she collected marsh marigolds and brought them into the house in Dromore Street for her mother. At that time, in country districts around Banbridge, people tied marsh marigolds in bunches and hung them from the door knocker of their houses to keep the fairies away.

A child in Dromore told me that her father always singed the shape of a cross on her pony's back on May Eve. He used a match to do so. The child did not know why her father did this but supposed the sign of the cross was a protection against evil. She could not think of any reason for having to protect horses against evil on May Day.

In Belfast an old tradition was observed every May Day. Young boys and girls, both Protestant and Catholic, used to go and collect yarrow from the bog meadows. This was reported in 'The Whig' newspaper. Unfortunately, according to 'The Whig', sectarian violence erupted in what had been a happy custom based on old fertility rites so that it died out by the 1880s.

Another interesting custom was enacted by small girls. This custom, like the mummers, was very territorial. If two groups met they fought.

The girls choose a May Queen. The May Queen was usually fairly athletic and was able to obtain the necessary costume. She dressed up in crepe paper, or lace curtains, donned a crown and carried the decorated shaft of a brush.

Valerie Hall remembers being a May Queen in the Donegall Pass area of Belfast in the mid-1950s and her mother sitting up late at night using a sewing machine and crepe paper to make a costume, then decorating the shaft of a brush with crepe paper. Valerie says the brush shaft was very important and had to be carried horizontally.

I remember seeing a May Queen about the same period of time on the Castlereagh Road near the old Castle Cinema, which was at the junction between the Castlereagh Road and Clara Street. She was dressed in lace curtains with hundreds of shining beads hanging around her neck. The little girls around her sang:

> 'Our wee Queen can birl her leg,
> Birl her leg, birl her leg,
> Our wee Queen can birl her leg
> On a cold and frosty morning.'

The little queen, using a circular movement, threw her right leg as high in the air as she could and back down again, while her courtiers

Bonfire lit to celebrate St. John's Eve, Ulster Folk and Transport Museum 1990.

sang. The courtiers collected money which was divided out fairly among members of the group.

May is the month of Mary, Mother of Jesus. On May Eve she is thought to return to earth and walk around the countryside. In the past people scattered bluebells and marsh marigolds on the ground so she could walk on them. If they appeared flattened next day it was said that she had passed the house.

Dancing around a May-pole is an English tradition. It was not usual in Ireland. There is a Maypole in Holywood, County Down. I remember holding a coloured ribbon in my hand and dancing around it as a child. Strangers, like me, were made very welcome and a very nice gentleman directed the dancing in a kindly, humorous fashion so we knew what to do. As we danced round and round the Maypole the ribbons became shorter and shorter as they became wrapped around the pole. Eventually dancing became impossible because everyone was holding a short piece of ribbon against the pole. Everyone laughed and the dancing was reversed so that the pole was unwrapped. This custom is continued in Holywood to the present day.

Mid-Summer Day

The birthday of St. John the Baptist is celebrated on Mid-summer Day. The feast was marked by lighting bonfires on hilltops. Fires were also lit in front of the byre door and at country crossroads. People danced to music supplied by a fiddler and the custom of leaping the flames was common. Sometimes guns were fired into the air to frighten evil spirits. The Ulster Folk and Transport Museum celebrate St John's Eve each year by organising special events and lighting a bonfire in the grounds.

July 12th

The celebrations of July 12th commemorate King William the Third's victory at the battle of the Boyne in 1690. They are sectarian and Protestant in nature, ignoring the historical fact that the Pope was an unofficial supporter of King William! Bonfires are lit in Protestant areas on the eleventh night, people may dance around them although they are more likely to sit, or stand nearby drinking, singing sectarian songs and 'cracking'. Strangers visiting a bonfire are treated in a friendly, hospitable manner and the 'crack' is usually

Lambeg Drum, Sandy Row, Eleventh Night, Belfast 1990.

good. I know many Catholics who join their Protestant friends for the eleventh night celebrations and the marches held on the following day. They really enjoy themselves!

Members of the Orange Order march on the 12th July. They carry banners and are accompanied by bands so that this is one of the most colourful and festive days in the calendar in Northern Ireland. The 12th July may be contrasted with 15th August, the Feast of the Assumption of the Virgin Mary which, for Roman Catholics, is an important feast day with religious services, outings and in Ulster an opportunity to display sectarian emblems.

Lammas

Lammas Day was celebrated either on the last Sunday in July or the first Sunday in August, The name 'Lammas' is derived from

Lughnasa, meaning start of harvest. Lughnasa is called after the ancient pagan god of harvest, Lugh, who was Cuchulain's father.

At harvest time young people were permitted to go together unchaperoned. Another ancient god, called Pilgra, is also celebrated at this time so young people were sent on pilgrimages. It is traditional to visit the Holy Well at Belcoo, there is the great annual pilgrimage to Croagh Patrick in which several thousand people take part. However, for most people the great event was the pilgrimage to gather bilberries. Many a man met his wife for the first time while on an unchaperoned pilgrimage to gather bilberries.

Lammas is the time for fairs such as that held each year in Ballycastle, the Auld Lammas Fair and the Puck Fair, in Killorglin.

Harvest

September and October are farmers' busiest months. Friends, neighbours and paid labourers banded together to help each other bring in the harvest before the invention of machines. They moved from farm to farm until the work was done. There was usually a gay and boisterous atmosphere because people were together for a long period of time and there was a mixing of old and young of both sexes.

Auld Lammas Fair, Ballycastle, August 1989.

Making hay while the sun shines. Ulster Folk and Transport Museum, July 1990.

One of the most interesting events in the harvest was the cutting of the last sheaf, which was also called the 'hare' or the Calliagh. The women, who usually acted as binders, plaited the last small amount of growing corn and tied its top with a few straws. Reapers and binders then danced around the hare until someone called out 'Cut her down.' The reapers and sometimes the women as well marked out a distance of approximately six yards and one by one threw their hooks at the hare in an attempt to sever it with a single stroke.

When the hare was cut it could be hung up in the house or the barn to bring luck with the following harvest. Sometimes it was plaited into wisps which were hung in the barn or given away on New Year's Eve. The hare could also serve as decoration in the local Church Harvest Festival.

Once the harvest was gathered the workers were treated to a special meal, sometimes called the Churn. After the Churn there was a barn dance. This took place at each farm as the harvest was completed so people had a hectic social life during harvest time.

Hallowe'en

Hallowe'en marked the end of the farming year and the beginning of winter so it was a very important festival.

According to folk lore the supernatural world has the greatest power then to influence the life of humans. As a child I always dressed up at Hallowe'en and went outside with my friends to frighten ghosts away. Sometimes we pretended we were ghosts and played a game described as 'thunder and lightning' in other words we knocked on doors like thunder and ran away like lightning. We hoped that people answering the door would think that a ghost had visited the house!

We had a very cross neighbour who objected to us playing street games outside his house. When we played ball games he used to come and take our ball. We felt this was very unfair because we were always careful to confine the ball to the street and keep it out of the gardens. We got our revenge at Hallowe'en. Emboldened by our disguises we repeatedly knocked upon his door and ran away. The gentleman's name was Mr. Hoey so we stood outside his house and shouted:

'Old Hoey
Sat on his po-ey.'

as well as anything else we considered rude that came to mind.

We enjoyed making a bonfire and dancing around it. We always had fireworks and took particular delight in letting off 'bangers'. Once we lit a 'banger' and threw it into 'Old Hoey's' house through the letter box. We were very repentant when we realised how dangerous our action was. Fireworks were forbidden after 1969 when the Army was called into Northern Ireland because our much loved 'bangers' sounded like gunfire and the troups found them disconcerting. After that time fireworks were confined to official displays organised by such official bodies as District Councils.

We believed that the dead walked around on Hallowe'en night and that they could take revenge on the living. We were warned never to look behind us if we heard footsteps because if we caught the eye of the dead we ourselves would surely die. I do not think we took that threat seriously because we definitely looked behind us to see if 'Old Hoey' was chasing us. Sometimes he was!

Children still dress up at Hallowe'en, they still make lanterns out of turnips and play practical jokes. A favourite joke today appears to be to remove garden gates and hide them somewhere in the garden.

Calendar Customs still form an integral part of life in Ireland although in the North many people stopped observing the old traditions during the Second World War. Blackout, introduced to give protection from German bombers, made it inadvisable to light bonfires at the appropriate times during the year. People were too busy with the war effort to have time to observe all but the most important festivals. Increasing scientific knowledge means there is less superstition so there is no real reason, in that sense, for carrying on the old traditions. However, many families enjoy carrying out the old customs. It can be fun, gives a sense of unity and reminds us that there is more to life than materialism.

There are amazing differences in observation of traditional customs in different areas.

ACKNOWLEDGEMENTS

It is always pleasant to remember the many people who so generously gave help.

Sincere thanks are due to the Staff of The Ulster Folk and Transport Museum, especially Bill Crawford, Linda Ballard, Philip Robinson, Deidre Brown, Andrew Anderson, Deborah McAuley, Jonathan Bell, Mervyn Watson, Ken Anderson and Michael Donnelly.

I am also indebted to Dara Vallelly, the Armagh Rhymers; John Gilmore and Evelyn Cardwell, The Ulster American Folk Park; Tony Canavan, The Federation of Ulster Local Studies; Valerie Hall, Institute of Irish Studies, Queen's University Belfast; Jean Kelly, Benburb Centre; Tom Collins, Dungannon Multi-purpose Centre; Elizabeth McWaters, University Bookshop, Alwyn Corrin, Fairfields Bookshop; Anne Tannahill, Blackstaff Press.

Hal Crowe, Editor 'Farm Week', provided valuable information as did Colm Barton and Deidre McNully, Southern Education and Library Board; Elizabeth Harkin, The History Park, County Tyrone, Brian Lambkin; Heather Crawford; Frances Shaw; Charles McCourt; Ernest Scott; Nigel Jess; Di Watson; George Bryson; Betty Quinn; Lil McCusker, Jim Holland, Cahal Dallat, Roy Hamilton, Noelle and Graham Millar, Robert Bell, Maureen Armstrong and Marie Ward.

Thanks are due to my husband, George, Pat Meads and Lance Macmanaway who edited the text.

My daughter, Leona, and son, John, gave unlimited support. I am grateful to them.

I am indebted to Margaret and Robert Boston for permission to photograph their home, Laurelvale; to David Bryans, Banbridge Camera Club, for permission to reproduce his photograph of my father, Bill Henry; to the Ulster American Folk Park for permission to reproduce photographs of their replica of an 'emigrant' ship; to Rowel Friers for his cartoon of me; to George Hall of Hallographics for advice on the production of this book and to Ray MacCullough who designed the cover.

FURTHER READING

'Dear Uncle'. Immigrant letters to Antrim from the U.S.A., pub. Antrim and District Historical Society 1989.

'The Great Hunger'. Cecil Woodham-Smith, pub. Hamish Hamilton Ltd. 1962.

'Farming in Ulster'. Jonathan Bell and Mervyn Watson, pub. Friars Bush Press 1988.

'Ulster Farm and Food'. Activity Pack, Doreen McBride and Jonathan Bell, pub. Ulster Folk and Transport Museum 1989.

'Ulster Folk and Transport Museum Activity Guide'. Doreen McBride, ed. Deidre Brown and A. Anderson, pub. Longmans 1989. Available from Ulster Folk and Transport Museum.

'Irish Folk Ways'. E. Estyn Evans, pub. Routledge Kegan Paul Ltd 1957.

'Quaint Irish Customs and Superstitions'. Lady Wilde, pub. Mercier Press 1988

'Irish Folk History'. Henry Glassie, pub. The O'Brien Press, Dublin 1982.

'Old Days Old Ways'. Olive Sharkey, pub. The O'Brien Press 1985

'Irish Country Cures'. Patrick Logan, pub. Appletree Press 1981.

'An Irish Herbal'. The Botanalogical Universalis Hibernica John K'Eogh, edited Michael Scott, pub. The Aquarian Press 1986 (First published 1735).

'In Search of Biddy Early' Edmund Lenihan, pub. Mercier Press 1987.

'Irish Fairy and Other Folk Tales'. edited by W. B. Yeats, pub. Walter Scott Ltd. London.

'Rooms of Time'. Cahal Dallat, Faith Gibson, pub. Friars Bush Press 1988.

'The Hearth and Stool and All!'. Kevin Danaher, pub. Mercier Press 1985.

INDEX